RETIRING TO SPAIN

Women's narratives of nostalgia, belonging and community

Anya Ahmed

First published in Great Britain in 2015 by

Policy Press
University of Bristol
1-9 Old Park Hill
Bristol
BS2 8BB
UK
t: +44 (0)117 954 5940
pp-info@bristol.ac.uk
www.policypress.co.uk

North America office:
Policy Press
c/o The University of Chicago Press
1427 East 60th Street
Chicago, IL 60637, USA
t: +1 773 702 7700
f: +1 773 702 9756
sales@press.uchicago.edu
www.press.uchicago.edu

© Policy Press 2015

British Library Cataloguing in Publication Data
A catalogue record for this book is available from the British Library

Library of Congress Cataloging-in-Publication Data
A catalog record for this book has been requested

ISBN 978 1 447313 304 hardcover

The right of Anya Ahmed to be identified as author of this work has been asserted by her in
accordance with the Copyright, Designs and Patents Act 1988.

Cover design by Policy Press
Front cover image: istock/Shutterstock
Printed and bound in Great Britain by CPI Group (UK) Ltd,
Croydon, CR0 4YY
Policy Press uses environmentally responsible print partners

For Dan, for every little and big thing

Contents

Acknowledgements   vi
Preface   viii

One   Retiring to the Costas: British women's narratives of   1
           nostalgia, belonging and community

Part 1: Lives in context
Two   Conceptualising, theorising and narrating retirement   17
           migration
Three   Locating the women: macro, meso and micro contexts   35
Four   Boundary spanning and reconstitution: retirement   51
           migration and the search for community

Part 2: Lived experiences
Five   Leaving the UK: motives, agency and decision-making   65
           processes
Six   Living in Spain: 'idyllisation' and realisation   87
Seven   Belonging to networks: reconciling agency and   105
           positionalities
Eight   Renegotiating family relationships: managing intimacy   129
           from a distance
Nine   Locating 'home' and community: the end point of plot   147
           movement

Conclusion
           Nostalgia, belonging and community: linking   161
           time and space

Afterword   167
Notes   169
References   173
Index   193

Acknowledgements

The work for this book began over ten years ago and there are many people to whom I owe a huge debt of gratitude for their support, wisdom, encouragement and advice along the way. First I want to thank the women in Spain for taking part in my research, and for involving me in their lives, in particular, of course, Vera and Deidre for their hospitality, kindness, generosity and friendship.

My thanks go to Bogusia Temple who was there at the very beginning when I was thinking about undertaking a PhD and throughout my studies at the University of Central Lancashire. Bogusia introduced me to narrative analysis, has always challenged and inspired me and is now a valued friend. Thanks, too, to Nicky Stanley, whose painstaking attention to my drafts helped me develop as a writer. I must also extend gratitude to Annie Huntingdon for her insightful comments. Thanks to Graham Crow for suggesting that I write the book and to Peter Dwyer for encouraging me to actually do it and for giving feedback on the proposal. Thanks also to Karen O'Reilly for taking the time to discuss my ideas for the book. Thank you also to the reviewers of the proposal and of the final book.

I am very grateful to the commissioning editors at the Policy Press, Emily Watt and Isobel Bainton, for their enthusiasm about the book and their help throughout the publishing process.

Many, many thanks, too, to Louise Ackers, Chris Coey, Angela Cotton, Vanessa May, Debbie Millard and Julie Morton for their helpful comments on drafts of chapters and also for their encouragement. I also owe thanks to my colleagues in the School of Nursing, Midwifery, Social Work and Social Sciences at the University of Salford, in particular Karen Kinghorn and Steve Myers, the Knowledge and Place research group, and the Sustainable Housing and Urban Studies Unit. I owe a debt of gratitude to Alison Brettle and Paula Ormandy for their support and humour in the difficult times of writing.

On a personal note, heartfelt thanks to my own 'community' for your love, giving me a sense of belonging and for believing in my abilities. First my family: my dad Abdi, my late mum Eunice, sister Alison and brother-in-law Bazill Ahmed Barrett; Aunty Win Andrews; my parents-in-law, Angela and Anthony Peacock, and the rest of the Peacocks; Mathew, Sally, Nancy and Kitty; and Edward and Jo. To my friends too, Julia Lucas, Race and Andy Williams, Val Alker and Pete Luddon, Lisa Beber, and Tony and Hilary Newman: thank you.

Thanks also to Debbie Latimer, Asha Abdillahi, Hannah Cameron, Ubah Egal, Kiona Simpson and Ruth Webber.

Finally, 'thanks' doesn't come close to capturing the depth of gratitude I feel to my husband, Dan: for your support throughout the highs and lows of writing, particularly in the final stages when my lovely mum died; for your unwavering belief in me; for taking on the cat; for the fun and laughter; and for being you.

Preface

In November 2000 I was visiting my friends Vera and Deidre at their house in Yorkshire, when Vera announced that they planned to retire early and move to the Costa Blanca in Spain the following year. Since the 1970s, they had taken regular holidays there and I was aware that they had recently visited again. What I didn't know was that this trip was actually an 'inspection visit' organised by an agent who sold houses to the British market on behalf of property developers in Spain. My friends excitedly told me about their plans, imagining a future life where they would stroll along the beach in the evenings before going out in search of tapas and Rioja. Deirdre was particularly rapturous about having the opportunity to paint again, while Vera had a long list of places of cultural interest that she had always wanted to visit, but never had enough time to on holiday. They talked about the charms of the nearest town, Torrevieja, which they planned to frequent when they moved and they also looked forward to learning Spanish and getting to know 'the locals'. Listening to my friends talk and hearing about their future plans, I became increasingly enthusiastic, especially when they extended an open invitation to me: I was welcome to visit any time I wanted for as long as I liked. They had already 'done their research' and informed me that there were several affordable flights a day from Manchester (where I lived) to Alicante, the nearest airport, and that the journey would take just over two hours.

Vera and Deidre moved to the Costa Blanca in May 2001, and I visited them there for the first time in August of that year. Although their house was a 20-minute walk from the Mediterranean coast, rather than the imagined stroll through pleasant Spanish landscape, the route to the sea was through vast building sites and scrubland. The roads were unfinished, there was no public transport, and the whole area was very much a work in progress, and far from the Spanish paradise they envisaged. On my first visit I took a boat from Torrevieja to Cabo Roig, and was amused to overhear a game being played by a young boy and his father who were counting the cranes along the coast. There were dozens dotted along the coast line, evidence of rapid and haphazard house-building characterised by a lack of planning (Huete et al, 2008). Migration to this costa was gaining momentum.

Vera and Deirdre were also surprised and disappointed to find themselves living in 'estates packed with fellow country-men [sic]' (Mantecon and Huete, 2007, 327): almost all of the residents on their 'urbanisation' were British, with only one Spanish family, from

Madrid, who had bought a second home there. However, at this point they were still very optimistic about their new life and anticipated that once the area was completed their Mediterranean idyll would materialise. They had already made several friends and had also joined a 'ladies' club',[1] and I met many of them on my first visit. All of these women had moved to Spain from the UK, most of them recently and all were unanimous in praising their new life there. Much of their talk centred on the 'sense of community' which they felt had been revived in Spain, and they made frequent comparisons to the lack of community characterising life in the UK and expressed relief and joy at having found it again. Encouraged by Vera and Deidre, I visited again in December 2001 and at the Silver Ladies' Christmas party, found myself having similar conversations about community and its decline in the UK. It was fascinating to hear about the women's motivations to move to Spain and their subsequent experiences and to note that their nostalgic recollections of past 'communities' in the UK often precluded their own experiences and memories and preceded their lifetimes.

At this time I had been working in Higher Education for about five years, mainly teaching and undertaking contract research. I had been thinking for some time about beginning doctoral research but couldn't quite settle on a topic. Much of the contract research I was involved with focused on immigration to the UK and the experiences of migrants in their new country. Inspired by a re-reading of Valerie Karn's (1977), *Retiring to the seaside*, and a research project I'd been involved in in Oldham and Rochdale at the time of the 2001 riots, I later became very aware of what Irene Hardill (2006) describes as an 'ironic parallel'. There was a media, policy and political preoccupation with migration to the UK and the cohesion and integration of minority groups, but much less attention seemed to be paid to the large numbers of British people who were moving abroad. Also, at the same time, the New Labour government appeared to be obsessed with 'community' and its revival, to solve the problems associated with ethnic diversity in the UK. On my third visit to Spain in May 2002, it was becoming apparent that for some of the women I had previously met, the Mediterranean idyll was not living up to expectations and many, including Vera and Deirdre planned to return to the UK. This disillusionment with Spain was also framed in terms of 'community' and but was now voiced regarding non-belonging and dislocation while there. Of course, these women were not a persecuted minority group struggling to survive, but there was a strong sense that their determined cohesion and talk of community was, for many, a strategy to enable them to thrive.

So my interest in retirement migration was very much influenced and underpinned by my interest in community and belonging. Social world observations ignited my sociological imagination and then I developed and employed a conceptual repertoire to frame explanations of community and belonging in retirement migration. This formed the basis of my (part-time) doctoral project. Over a four-year period, from 2001 to 2004, over 11 visits, I spent just under a year in Spain and conducted in-depth narrative interviews with 17 case studies from 2003–04. Part of this research was submitted as a PhD thesis in 2010 (Ahmed, 2010) and this and additional data has been re-analysed taking account of broader and more recent theoretical developments to form this book. Simply put, my focus here is on why community is still so important to people, how it represents belonging to different 'things' at different times and how this illuminates aspects of social change and continuity from particular vantage points. Exploring how a group of mainly working-class women from the UK search for, construct, imagine, symbolise, evoke and experience (or not) belonging and community in their retirement, provides the opportunity to consider what this represents from different perspectives in new contexts.

Anya Ahmed
Salford, January 2015

Retiring to the Costas: British women's narratives of nostalgia, belonging and community

> Nostalgics from all over the world would find it difficult to say what exactly they yearn for – St Elsewhere, another time, a better life. (Svetlana Boym, 2001, xiv)

This book focuses on the lives of a group of women from the UK who moved to the Costa Blanca[1] in Spain in retirement. We follow their journeys as they seek 'community' and belonging in a world characterised by rapid social change. Imbued with nostalgic yearning, community is hailed as a panacea to the ills of modernity and as a representation of social continuity. Nostalgia denotes the mourning of a lost home or place and a lost time – and in this way – the search for community and belonging can also be understood as a quest for another epoch. For many of these women, migrating in retirement symbolises a movement back in time as well as across space: they moved to Spain to escape Britain in an uncertain present, and to return to an imagined 'England' of the past. Women's different migration trajectories are disaggregated, considering return migration to the UK alongside permanent settlement in Spain and temporary residence, allowing for further exploration of what community and belonging mean to people in different contexts at different times, and how the search for community and belonging for some, also shape decisions to return 'home'. The women featured imagine and create their own solutions to feelings of dislocation, both in the UK and in Spain, against the backdrop of policy and political uses of community in the UK.

Retiring to the Costas

Over the last 30 years and during the first decade of the new millennium in particular, retirement to the Spanish coastal resorts (costas) has been increasing. Globalisation, economic growth and EU enlargement following the Maastricht Treaty in 1992, allowing nationals to settle and buy properties (Warnes et al, 2004; Janoschka, 2011; Huete and

Mantecon, 2012) have all been significant in shaping the expansion of new forms of migration. Additionally, speculative purpose-built housing development, stimulated by house price inflation from the mid-1980s in Europe, coupled with the rise in estate agents for international markets have been important in creating residential estates known as *urbanizaciones* for British migrants in Spain (Casado-Díaz, 2006). Retirement migration is usually from the north to the south, where the climate is warmer (Blaakilde and Nilsson, 2013), and coastal areas have historically been associated with hedonism and a holiday atmosphere (Bell et al, 2004). Retired northern Europeans move to Spain for an imagined 'Mediterranean lifestyle' (Huete, 2009, cited in Huete and Mantecon, 2012), and the Costa Blanca in particular is populated by large numbers of people who have bought a 'place in the sun'.[2] In the first decade of the twenty-first century, there were more houses sold to foreign nationals than to Spanish people (Huete and Mantecon, 2012), although migration to this costa has a shorter history than migration to the Costa del Sol (O'Reilly, 2003; 2007a; Ahmed, 2011). Factors influencing the rise in retirement migration include: increased life expectancy and positive ageing in early old age; rises in the consumption and purchasing power of older people in the EU; increased residential mobility; and rising aspirations (Casado-Díaz, 2006; King et al, 1998; Rodriguez et al, 1998; Warnes et al, 2004). Previously the preserve of an elite demographic (Casado-Díaz et al, 2004; Casado-Díaz, 2006; Benson, 2011a; 2011b), retirement migration has now become accessible to a wider range of people (Huete and Mantecon, 2012) and the women featured would be among the first generation of working-class people to experience the benefits of mass tourism and cheap air travel (Ahmed, 2011). Examining these women's experiences of migration in retirement then, provides a unique opportunity for less-heard voices to emerge.

British people also move to Spain in retirement to take advantage of a better climate, slower pace of life, lower cost of living and to benefit from available amenities and social and practical opportunities, for example, the presence of compatriots and the fact that English is widely spoken (see King et al, 1998; 2000; O'Reilly, 2003; Rodriguez et al, 1998; Huete and Mantecon, 2012). Tourist infrastructures and transport links facilitate easy movement abroad (King et al, 1998) and mass tourism facilitates migration flows (Williams and Hall, 2002; Casado-Díaz et al, 2004; O'Reilly, 2000a; 2007a): the Costa Blanca has been described as a 'paradigmatic example of mass tourism' (Huete et al, 2008, 153). Retirement migration destinations are therefore influenced by previous tourism and there are links between destinations which have become familiar over time, and places where people choose to live in in retirement (Warnes et al, 2004). It follows then, that the destinations that people choose, tells us about the lives they want to lead post-migration (Warnes et al, 2004); and importantly, also about the lives they led before, as I will explore.

Retirement migration represents a new lifestyle in retirement and needs to be understood within the context of structural, cultural and demographic change in society. Migration happens because of social change and it also causes social change, and to fully understand these macro vicissitudes we also need to take account of human agency (Van Hear, 2010) and how people experience and adjust to such processes. Within the context of wider structures and through the lens of community and belonging, I consider how retired women's agency and experiences are facilitated and circumscribed by their 'positionalities' and how these intersect or 'translocate'. Taking account of recent theoretical developments in migration research (Lutz, 2010; King, 2012a) – in terms of linking macro, meso and micro levels to understand the social processes involved in migration (O'Reilly, 2012) – my study of narrative nostalgia, belonging and community presents a new theoretical locus for understanding retirement migration. Focusing on retirement migration as a form of social change through a structural narrative analytical framework brings new perspectives in theorising gendered, age-related and ethnic and class positionalities, and how they shape community construction in new contexts. Considering women's narratives of community as counter-narratives (Andrews and Bamberg, 2004) to the meta-narrative of the UK government's use of community highlights how imaginations of the past can potentially solve problems of non-belonging in the present.

My decision to conduct research with retired migrant women was influenced by there being very limited research on the experiences of older women in migration; therefore my sampling strategy was theoretically informed (Glaser and Strauss, 1967) and purposive (Mason, 2002). Since the 1960s, feminists have criticised the limited perspectives of quantitative and positivist accounts of migration for being gender blind and they have drawn attention to: 'The invisibility of women on the map of migration' (Anthias and Cederberg, 2006, 15). This 'invisibility' can be explained in part by a historical focus on men's experiences being perceived as 'natural' in migration research, an absence of female scholars, and the fact that women migrants are conceptualised as following men or behaving like them (Lutz, 2010). However, there is now a growing body of literature on the topic of gender and migration (see Borkert et al, 2006; Zlotnik, 2003;

Anthias and Cederberg, 2009; Ryan and Webster, 2008; Hoang, 2011; Lundstrom, 2014), and gender, along with other social divisions shape migration experiences producing 'multiple realities of migration' (Borkert et al, 2006, 3). Gender specific migration experiences are important since migration is not gender neutral (Boyd and Grieco, 2003): women's migration experiences are structurally and qualitatively different from men (Anthias et al, 2012). However, another influencing factor guiding the research was that I had access to a group of women through my contacts in Spain; therefore this was also a convenience sample.

I now introduce the reader to the women upon whose experiences of migration in retirement this book is based. All names indicated are pseudonyms.

Introducing the women

Agatha

Agatha aged 60, was born in the north of England and had lived there all of her life, prior to moving to Spain. She and her husband bought a holiday home in the Costa Blanca four years ago, moving out to live full time six months previously when they both retired. Both Agatha and her husband had already applied for *residencia*[3] and planned to live in Spain permanently. Agatha finished secondary school and began work aged 16. Before retiring, she worked part time in social care while her husband was employed in printing. She has three sons and five grandchildren, all living in close proximity to where she lived in the UK.

Agnes

Born in the Home Counties, Agnes, aged 69, moved to Spain on a full-time basis with her second husband two years ago. Agnes finished secondary school and previously worked part time and full time in retail, and had retired several years previously. Prior to retiring, her husband was an engineer and was from a Scandinavian country. Agnes and her husband lived in Scandinavia for five years during the 1970s, returning to live in Norfolk in 1978 where they had lived ever since. Although they originally planned to live permanently in Spain, they now wanted to return to the UK. Agnes has two daughters and a son and four grandchildren living several hundred miles away from where she lived in the UK. She also has two stepchildren and four step-grandchildren living in Scandinavia.

Bernice

Aged 62, Bernice and her husband bought a holiday home in Spain three years previously and spent approximately a third of the year there. They planned to maintain this arrangement for the foreseeable future as they were happy with living part time in Spain and the UK. Bernice was born and lived all of her life in the north-east of England. Bernice finished secondary school and both she and her husband worked full time in manufacturing and retail prior to retiring. They have two daughters and a son and six grandchildren, all of whom live in the north-east of England.

Deidre

Originally from the north-west of England, Deidre, aged 62, was in a relationship with Vera and they moved to Spain together two years previously. Deidre had been married twice before, her first husband was an accountant and they lived in Peru for six years before their divorce. Several years later she married a second husband, a widower, who was an academic; and she became a full-time stepmother to his three sons. Deidre went on to further education following secondary school and gained A-level qualifications, although she did not engage in paid employment until she was in her 40s. She worked part time in a bookshop and then part time in a university library prior to moving to Spain. When they moved to Spain Deidre and Vera planned to stay for approximately ten years but had since decided to return to the north of England where they had lived before to moving to Spain.

Celia

Celia moved to Spain with her husband two years previously. Aged 59, she and her husband took early retirement in the UK. Celia was born and lived in the north of England for the whole of her life prior to moving to Spain. She finished secondary school and worked part time in retail, while her husband worked in construction. They planned to live in Spain permanently and had *residencia*. She has one daughter and a granddaughter living in the UK, several hundred miles away from where she had lived previously. Celia, along with Cynthia, established the Silver Ladies club.

Cynthia

Cynthia is 54 years old and has been living in Spain full time for the last three years, although she and her husband owned their home there for five years. From the north-east of England, Cynthia and her husband planned to live in Spain permanently and had *residencia*. Cynthia finished secondary school and prior to retiring she worked part time and full time in manufacturing and sales, while her husband worked in chemical manufacturing. Cynthia was the only woman who could speak sufficient Spanish to 'get by'. Cynthia has four children and eight grandchildren, most of who lived in the north-east in the UK. Cynthia was instrumental in setting up the Silver Ladies club.

Enid

Enid, aged 57 is from Northern Ireland. She and her husband bought a holiday home in Spain two years previously and spend approximately four to six months of each year there. However, they planned to sell this property and look elsewhere for a second home, either somewhere else in Spain or in another country. Enid went to university and prior to retirement was a teacher while her husband worked as a civil servant. She has two children, one of whom lived in the north-west of England and the other in Northern Ireland.

Jenny

Jenny, aged 56, has lived in Spain for two-and-a-half years and moved there with her second husband. She was born and lived in the south of England and has a daughter and granddaughter. She moved to Spain thinking that her daughter and her family would also be moving there to start a business but this had not happened. Jenny finished secondary school and worked full time in retail prior to moving to Spain, while her husband was previously an engineer.

Joy

Joy was 54 years old and had been living in Spain full time with her husband for two years, although they had owned a property there for five years. Joy finished secondary school and was a full-time homemaker, while her husband was previously an environmentalist for an oil company. Joy was originally from the south of England, but had lived in the south-west, south-east and Wales prior to moving to

Spain. She has twin boys both living in the south. Joy and her husband planned to stay in Spain and had *residencia*.

Lillian

Lillian, aged 61, and her husband had been living in Spain for just under a year but had owned their home for three years. They were undecided about whether to remain in the Costa Blanca full time or to keep their home as a holiday home and move further inland. Regardless, they planned to stay permanently in Spain and their eldest son planned to buy a holiday home close by. Both Lillian and her husband had *residencia*. Lillian finished secondary school and worked part time in retail prior to taking early retirement for health reasons; her husband was a builder and he had also taken early retirement on health grounds. Lillian was born and lived in the south-east of England for all of her life before moving to Spain. She has three sons and three grandchildren all living in the south-east in the UK.

Mabel

Mabel, a widow aged 83, had been living in Spain for a year. She was unusual in the research participants in that she was older, had been retired for over 20 years when she moved to Spain, and also in that she was from a more privileged background. Oxbridge educated, Mabel had worked in the teaching profession after serving in the armed forces (WRENs) in the Second World War. She lived in France following the war and married a French man, returning to the UK in 1947 with their son, following their divorce. She remarried in 1952 and was widowed for a second time in 1990. Her second husband was a civil servant and they lived in the south-west of England. Mabel planned to stay in Spain for the rest of her life and she had *residencia*.

Margot

Margot, aged 60, was divorced and moved to Spain alone a year ago. She was from the south of England and had lived there all of her life, apart from a brief period in her early 20s when she lived in Jersey. Margot finished secondary school and worked full time in manufacturing and retail. She has two daughters and a son and one granddaughter. Margot planned to stay in Spain permanently and had *residencia*. Margot's sister had a holiday home nearby which she visited for part of the year.

Myra

Aged 60, Myra was divorced and moved to Spain alone just over six months ago. Originally from the Midlands in England, she has a daughter and a granddaughter. Myra had lived in the Middle East for a brief period during the 1970s as her husband worked in the oil industry. Myra finished secondary school and prior to moving to Spain worked full time in retail. Myra planned to stay permanently and had applied for *residencia*.

Olive

Aged 57 and originally from south-east Asia, Olive moved to Germany to train as a nurse when she was 22 years old. While in Germany she met her British husband and subsequently moved to the UK where she lived for 33 years until their divorce. She lived in the north-west of England and worked in social care for 30 years. She has been living alone in Spain full time for two years and planned to remain there, having *residencia*, although she loosely planned to return to the country of her birth in her 'fourth age'. Olive has two children and four grandchildren residing in the north-west of England.

Phyllis

Aged 77, Phyllis and her husband moved to the Costa Blanca from the south-east England two years previously. Phyllis finished secondary school and she and her husband worked together in catering up until moving to Spain. She has a son and daughter-in-law who had already moved to the Costa Blanca and she planned to remain in Spain permanently and had *residencia*.

Vera

Aged 59, from Yorkshire and in a relationship with Deidre, Vera moved to Spain two years previously. She originally finished her education after secondary school, and worked in retail, but returned to higher education as a mature student. Following this, she worked in local government and the voluntary sector. Vera and Deidre originally planned to stay in Spain but had decided to return, although Vera had taken out *residencia*. Vera has one daughter who lives in the same area that she is from in the UK.

Viv

From the North Midlands, Viv, aged 54, and her husband bought a holiday home three years previously and spent half of the year in Spain and the remainder in England. Viv was happy with this arrangement, enjoying the best of both worlds, and they planned to retain their second home in Spain. Viv did not complete secondary school due to illness and has never been in paid employment. Viv has three sons and a daughter, all living close to where she lives in the UK.

These women can be classified as falling into five related but different residential categories: those living in Spain permanently, that is without a home in the UK, who wished to remain there (Celia, Cynthia, Mable, Agatha, Myra, Margot, Olive, Lillian and Phyllis); those living in Spain permanently who wished to return to the UK (Jenny, Agnes, Vera and Deirdre); those living in Spain permanently but are ambivalent about staying (Joy); those who lived in Spain for part of the year and were happy with this arrangement (Bernice and Viv) and finally, those who live in Spain for part of the year but did not wish to retain their home there (Enid).[4] Although typically elderly migrants are very mobile in earlier life (see Huber and O'Reilly, 2004), most of these women – apart from Myra, Mabel, Deidre and Olive – lived in the locale of their birth.

Knowing community and belonging in retirement migration: epistemological and methodological considerations

In 1993 Keith Halfacree and Paul Boyle made the case for using a biographical approach to make sense of migration, arguing that all aspects of migrants' lives influence migration decisions and experiences. Almost 20 years later, Russell King (2012a) criticised the artificial distinction made between the determinants and processes and patterns in migration by migration researchers, and suggested a life history approach as a solution. I see narrative research as a representation or feature of biographical research, related to the study of individuals and their lives in structural, cultural, temporal and spatial contexts. Narrating can also be understood as a mechanism through which people examine their lives and gain understanding of the social and material worlds (see Polkinghorne, 1988; Ricoeur, 1984; Plummer, 2001; and Bruner, 1990), and analysing narratives gives voice to the complexity of people's experiences (Skrbiš, 2008) in migration.

The term 'narrative' is derived from the Latin *gnarus,* and means 'knowing'. There is however, no consensus on what narrative 'is', or how narratives should be analysed (Ahmed, 2013). I define narrative as recorded, transcribed stories, which have become units for interpretation and a key feature distinguishing narratives is the implication that one event usually causes another, suggesting persuasiveness or coherence (Riessman, 2000a; 2003). An interpretivist epistemology shapes my approach to narrative and my view of narratives is that they are not 'ethnographic testimonials' (Ahmed, 2013); instead, they need to be analysed and interpreted since they are subjective, rooted in time, place and experience, are perspective ridden and linked to culture and history. Further, language is a cultural resource that people draw upon and it reflects and constructs the contexts in which people live (Temple, 2002; 2008a; Ahmed, 2011).

This book highlights important methodological and epistemological issues surrounding the role of perceptions in social research (Mah and Crow, 2011). Since we are agents influenced by our past experiences and positionalities, these, and multiple other factors influence our understanding and interpretations of the social world (Anthias, 2002). My approach here is that truth is multiple and subjective and ultimately an interpretation. Underscoring women's experiences and motivations, the powerful role of nostalgia in linking time and space in their narrative accounts of community and belonging in migration is examined in relation to the overlapping and reinforcing relationships between different forms of community. Drawing on Ricoeur's (1984) work on time and narrative and Bakhtin's (1981) use of the *chronotope*[5] in literature I aim to persuade the reader that nostalgia can be understood as a form of chronotope (Bakhtin, 1981) since it links a lost place and also a lost (past) time (Boym, 2001). I argue that nostalgia, like community, is symbolic and utilitarian (O'Reilly, 2000a) yet also ephemeral and intangible and can also be restorative or reflective (Boym, 2001). A thematic and structural narrative approach centring on the use of plot (Riessman, 1993), time (Roberts, 2004), positioning (Anthias, 2002; 2006) and an examination of linguistic devices (Czarniawska, 2004) provides linkage to and ethnographic understanding (Gubrium and Holstein, 1998) of the structural and material circumstances of women's lives, their positionalities and agency.

Having introduced the premise, focus and approach taken, I now provide a chapter-by-chapter summary. In the first part of the book the theoretical, epistemological, methodological contexts in which retired British women's migration is placed are established and I identify the particular structural, economic, temporal, demographic and cultural contexts enabling and framing their migration. The second part addresses women's lived experiences of migration; how and why the quest for belonging and community in Spain is successful for some and not for others, and how some women manage heterolocal lives (Halfacree, 2012).

Part 1: Lives in context

Chapter Two: Conceptualising, theorising and narrating retirement migration

In this chapter my approach to conceptualising and theorising retirement migration is presented and I discuss how the women in the study examine their lives (Ricoeur, 1984) through their narrative accounts. I explain how I use a thematic and structural narrative analytical approach to illuminate women's lived experiences of migration in retirement to provide ethnographic understanding of the structural and material circumstances of their lives.

Chapter Three: Locating the women: macro, meso and micro contexts

In Chapter Three, a discussion of the macro contexts framing retired women's migratory decisions in terms of 'upper structural layers' and 'more proximate structural layers' is presented (O'Reilly, 2000a). The focus then shifts to the 'meso context' or women's positionalities and I consider how positionalities act as a meso level of interaction between wider structures and women's agency. I explain my use of translocational positionality and discuss this in terms of gender, class, age and ethnicity in theoretical and lived contexts.

Chapter Four: Boundary spanning and reconstitution: retirement migration and the search for community

This chapter focuses on how constructions and experiences of community and belonging can illuminate processes of social change and continuity. Retirement migration is conceptualised as a form and consequence of social change and the relationship between community and belonging is unravelled. I discuss how community is thought to have been lost but can be regained, and highlight the role of the imagination and the imagery of the idyll in constructing it, arguing that nostalgia as a cultural resource plays a central role. My focus is on different forms of belonging to place, networks, identity or positionality and how these are useful to understand boundary spanning and reconstitution in the context of retirement migration.

Part 2: Lived experiences

Chapter Five: Leaving the UK: motives, agency and decision-making processes

In this chapter, I explore the reasons for women's dislocation in and from the UK, and their agency in decision-making processes in migrating to Spain. I consider how women present themselves through their narratives and how this illuminates household gender dynamics. Through the analytical use of plot, I also focus on 'the where', 'the whys' and 'the how' of retirement migration.

Chapter Six: Living in Spain: 'idyllisation' and realisation

In this chapter the focus on place continues but the context shifts to Spain. I consider how women experience and construct belonging and non-belonging and the complex relationships they have with place, highlighting that it can be imagined, pragmatic and contingent on experiences and intentions. Different experiences of living in Spain begin to emerge. Some women manage to overcome certain obstacles once there; others do not, while some women manage heterolocal lives in retirement.

Chapter Seven: Belonging to networks: reconciling agency and positionalities

This chapter begins by examining how social networks are constructed by people's agency and fulfil a necessary function while out of context. An exploration of how positionalities also shape networks is presented and an example of a 'ladies' club' is used to examine how British-run social clubs can be gendered. The role of language and its significance in terms of constructing and reflecting positionalities is explored and women's experiences of networks in Spain are discussed in terms of how, once in Spain, retired working-class British women find themselves again on the margins. I consider how English – rather than British – ethnic identities are constructed out of context and how these 'translocate' with other positionalities.

Chapter Eight: Renegotiating family relationships: managing intimacy from a distance

The focus of this chapter is on how women manage and negotiate family responsibilities in the UK. Drawing on theories of grandparenting styles and intergenerational solidarity, I explore how women reconcile, reject and reconceptualise traditional notions of being a mother and grandmother once they have left the UK and how this can sometimes be at odds with being a wife. Throughout this chapter it becomes evident through analysing narrative footing and positioning, that different migration trajectories and positions illuminate conflicting feelings, perceptions and experiences.

Chapter Nine: Locating 'home' and community: the end point of plot movement

Women's divergent migration trajectories are considered in relation to the end point of plot movement: the place where the women want to be and how they construct belonging and 'home'. I discuss how for some women, moving back to the UK represents the chance of a better life and the recovery of what was lost, while for those who wish to stay in Spain, it represents 'home'. For women living in two places, their experiences are of being 'betwixt and between'.

Conclusion: Nostalgia, belonging and community: linking time and space

The book concludes by revisiting the significance of studying nostalgia and 'community' in new contexts and highlights the enduring theoretical and practical significance of community. Examining how retired British women search for, imagine and experience belonging and community in Spain allows links to be made between micro, meso and macro levels and unravelling belonging and community facilitates understanding of social change and continuity. In the final analysis I premise that nostalgia and community helps us understand women's agency and positionalities within the material and structural circumstances of their lives.

In the following chapter I explain my approach to conceptualising, theorising and understanding retirement migration.

Part 1
Lives in context

TWO

Conceptualising, theorising and narrating retirement migration

Introduction

The focus of this chapter is on how I gain knowledge of the processes involved in constructing shifting and overlapping forms of belonging to different kinds of community and how this illuminates experiences of retirement migration. I begin by presenting a discussion of my conceptualisation of retirement migration and then unravel my approach to theory, explaining how women's experiences and agency are placed within wider structural contexts. I explore how understanding of retirement migration is gained through a thematic and structural narrative analytic approach centring on plot, time, identity or positionality and an analysis of linguistic devices employed. An important part of my approach to understanding women's experiences of belonging and community in retirement migration is the analytical use of nostalgia as a chronotope which I suggest links time and space in narrative. First, however, an outline of how I conceptualise retirement migration is presented.

Conceptualising retirement migration

Migration is complex and fluid (King, 2012a) and migration flows alter population totals and age-structures and affect settlement patterns (King et al, 1998). Research on British retirement migration to Europe has focused on Spain (O'Reilly, 2000a; Rodriguez et al, 1998; Oliver, 2008; Casado-Díaz, 2006); France (Benson, 2011a; 2011b); Malta (Warnes and Patterson, 1998); Italy (King et al, 2000); and Portugal (Williams and Patterson, 1998). Initially, retirement migration was placed within the context of population geography and migration studies, tourism and gerontology (King et al, 1998; 2000). There is a long debate about what is and is not migration, with some arguing that the idea of 'mobilities' (Urry, 2000) sidesteps this issue (King, 2012a). Mobilities captures the movement of people, ideas and information involving multiple places, and can be understood as embodying a continuum encompassing necessity and desire (Nagy and Korpela,

2013. In this way, migration can be understood within the context of 'economic and other opportunity differences' (De Haas, 2010, 1589). There are broadly three types of migration: the voluntary search for economic improvement; political exile or forced migration; and the choice of a different lifestyle (Geoffrey and Sibley, 2007). Retirees living in the Costa Blanca fall easily into the third category, but as has already been suggested, economic considerations influence the move to Spain, as do feelings of dislocation in the UK. Halfacree and Boyle (1993) influenced by Taylor (1969) and Beshers (1967) identify three types of migrant: first, purpose rational, where migration is considered and planned; second, traditional, when migration is linked to custom and habit; and third, hedonistic, when migration responds to immediate desires and feelings. However, although useful, these typologies are not so fixed in relation to the women featured as will become clear.

The movement of older people from one country to another has previously been labelled 'international retirement migration' (King et al, 2000), 'residential tourism' (O'Reilly, 2000a) and 'lifestyle migration' (Benson and O'Reilly, 2009). The term 'international retirement migration' has been used to differentiate between retirement migrations between countries and within the same country, and the women featured here also fit into this category. The term 'residential tourism' has also been widely used since the 1970s to capture two forms of mobility in Southern Europe: tourism and lifestyle migration (Huete and Mantecon, 2012). 'Residential tourism' is often used to describe housing developments in established tourist areas and is synonymous with second home ownership (Mantecon and Huete, 2007) and to describe a mix of permanent and temporary mobilities (van Noorloos, 2013). This term however, has been criticised by a number of researchers, mainly because it is seen as being contradictory since it categorises as tourists people who live permanently in tourist destinations. Further, the boundaries between tourism and migration are often blurred and this can also cause difficulties for the host society in terms of calculating population totals, particularly among second home owners (Huete and Mantecon, 2012). Spanish authorities classify Northern Europeans as residential tourists rather than immigrants, distinguishing them from non-EU (and non-white) migrants (O'Reilly, 2003). Additionally, in spite of a large amount of research being undertaken in a number of migration destinations into the causes, consequences and experiences of retirement migration, it remains difficult to quantify (Casado-Díaz et al, 2004). Geographically located on the outskirts of Spanish towns in a tourist destination, and on the periphery of the host society, in many ways the women in this study also could be accurately described as 'residential tourists', although they do not identify as tourists.

More recently, the concept 'lifestyle migration' (Benson and O'Reilly, 2009) has been used by a number of researchers to describe the movement of people from developed countries to improve their quality of life. Distinct from economic and forced migration, 'lifestyle migration' has resulted in much debate across a range of disciplines (Janoschka, 2011) and there is now a growing body of research and theory on this migration typology. 'Lifestyle migration' has been conceptualised as a quest (Benson, 2011a; 2011b) for a better life. Significantly though, as well as a search for a better life, crucially a quest also involves a search for something that is 'lost' (Ahmed, 2013). For the women featured, what is lost is community and belonging. Lifestyle migration embodies consumption and 'community' can also be understood as being one of the goods consumed (Benson and O'Reilly, 2009). Framed in terms of individualism (see Giddens, 1991; Beck 1992; Oliver, 2008; O'Reilly and Benson, 2009; Oliver and O'Reilly, 2010; Benson, 2011b) lifestyle migration encompasses the melding of several contingent factors: individual biographies and agency, structural and temporal pre-conditions and culturally significant imaginings (Benson and Osbaldiston, 2014). The concept 'lifestyle mobilities' (Duncan, Scott and Thulemark, 2013) has also recently been developed to frame mobility as an ongoing lifestyle choice and as a theoretical lens to illuminate the intersections of travel, leisure and migration.

Three different yet related types of lifestyle migration have been identified: residential tourists; rural idyll seekers and finally bourgeois bohemians (Benson and O'Reilly, 2009). Since the places which people choose as retirement destinations are influenced by their lifetime 'activity space' (King et al, 1998), the 'lifestyle migration' concept is useful as it situates the life post-migration within the context of the life before (O'Reilly and Benson, 2009). Drawing on Bourdieu's theories of lifestyle, consumption practices and social position, 'lifestyle migration' encapsulates the circumstances of people's lives before migration and how these influence migration choices, motivations and experiences of life within the migration destination (O'Reilly and Benson, 2009). The 'lifestyle migration' concept is also useful to capture the experiences of the women in this book since it has a past and present and a time/space dimension, and is one which I have previously employed elsewhere (see Ahmed 2011; 2012; 2013). However, the concept is not without critics, particularly in terms of its usefulness for quantitative research, since it is difficult to identify meaningful empirical characteristics beyond ethnic group as an analytical category (Huete et al, 2013). However, some migration researchers argue that using national frameworks to analyse migration is a problem with migration scholarship in general, rather than with lifestyle migration in particular (Levitt, 2012). For my purposes though, this does not pose a problem, since the women in my study in part represent an ethnic group, and this has relevance for my analysis of their experiences. 'Lifestyle migration' is also criticised for its subjectivity, lack of precision and the downplaying of economic considerations across mobility patterns (Huete et al, 2013). Here, women's subjective experiences are of central importance to my analysis, although I place their experiences in relevant wider contexts. The terms international retirement migrant, residential tourist and lifestyle migrant capture aspects of the women's migratory contexts and experiences. Women who live in both the UK and Spain can also be described as 'heterolocal' (Halfacree, 2012). The women's mobility can be understood as migration in retirement for a different lifestyle, informed by the one lived before. What is important is that I am not presenting 'retirement migration' as a simple typology to explain their mobility (Halfacree and Boyle, 1993); rather, as will become evident, this life course juncture has a structural, temporal, demographic and cultural significance which I unravel and relate to women's positionalities.

Theorising retirement migration

Migration crosses a range of disciplines and includes researchers from multiple theoretical epistemological, ontological and methodological positions. Across the social sciences there is a consensus that migration and mobility are of fundamental importance for understanding the dynamics of societies and social relations (King and Smith, 2012). However, disciplinary boundaries have created some difficulties in the development of migration theory (Castles, 2010). Theories of international migration can be split into a number of phases (King, 2012b): up to the 1960s push/pull and neo-classical approaches (based on Ravenstein's (1885) 'laws' of migration, focusing on rational choice and labour were dominant. This was followed by historical structural models, influenced by Marx and world capitalist systems theories; political economy models; then systems and network theories. By the 1980s new economies of migration theory were at the forefront, followed by the transnational or cultural turn from the 1990s onwards.[1] My approach to theorising retirement migration is located in the cultural turn which attempts to capture the significance of factors other than economic rational ones (King, 2002) and embeds migration in global processes and structures and in the context of migrants' life courses (Halfacree and Boyle, 1993; King, 2012b). Further, theories of tourism, lifestyle, ageing, place, community and identity (see O'Reilly, 2000a; Oliver, 2008; Benson, 2011a) have shaped previous accounts of retirement migration. However, it is worth noting that: 'migration is too diverse and multi-faceted to be explained in a single theory' (King, 2012b: 11; also see Osbaldiston, 2014). Although there are now numerous descriptive and explanatory accounts of motivations and experiences of retirement migration (see O'Reilly, 2000a; Oliver, 2008; Benson, 2011a) it is necessary to provide some such detail here since little has been written on working-class women's lives and on return migration[2] alongside decisions to remain in the migration destination.

The difficulties in developing migration theory across disciplinary boundaries are further compounded by migration research being characterised by binaries, one of the most obvious being the structure/agency debate (King, 2012a). As a consequence, unravelling the relationship between structure and agency has become a theoretical preoccupation in migration research and one which needs to be addressed (King, 2012b). Although structuration theory (Giddens, 1986) is useful for looking at the interplay between structure and agency – or the relationship between context and people's actions – it has limitations. Some theorists overly focus on the deterministic role of structures, others emphasise the transcendental nature of agency, while some researchers acknowledge the relationship between structure and agency without really illuminating their interaction in particular contexts (Bakewell, 2010).

A number of conditions which need to be addressed to develop a satisfactory theory of migration have been identified by migration researchers and I will be drawing on a combination of Massey et al's (1998), Bakewell's (2010),[3] and O'Reilly's (2012) approaches to develop a 'theoretical brick' (Bakewell, 2010, 1703) to explicate women's search for community and belonging in the context of retirement migration. Although each of these researchers differently present their theoretical framework, they share a focus on the importance of understanding structures, migrant's agency and the meso levels of interaction between them. To summarise, Massey et al's (1998) basic elements involve a consideration of the structural factors facilitating migration and people's motivation to migrate; Bakewell's (2010) focus is on people, places and temporality – in other words – who moves, where they move to – or not – and when; while O'Reilly (2012), drawing on Bourdieu (1977), Giddens (1986) and Stones (2005), highlights the importance of understanding the interaction between structures (external upper/ proximate and internal), habitus, practices and outcomes in developing a 'practice theory' of migration. Karen O'Reilly (2014) suggests that practice theory provides an ontological basis for understanding the relationship between structure and agency in migration, although account also needs to be taken of the 'social imaginary' both in terms of structure and agency (also see Benson, 2012).

I am not, however, claiming to develop a complete practice theory. I explain below how through thematic and structural narrative analysis, I am able to examine women's migration experiences within the wider structural contexts framing their agency, and also unravel the significance of their unique biographies (Benson, 2012). I discuss how a focus on plot, time and positionalities[4] provides an opportunity to investigate practices and outcomes while also taking account of temporality. I suggest that nostalgia as a device linking time and space in narrative, further illuminates retired women's experiences and constructions of community, belonging and non-belonging in migration.

Narrating retirement migration

People render their lives meaningful through narratives (Polkinghorne, 1988) and narrating allows for an examination of one's life (Ricoeur, 1984). Narrative accounts are useful to gain insight into how individuals understand and interpret their place in the world, particularly in relation to belonging (Anthias, 2002). Women who move from the UK to Spain examine their lives through recounting nostalgic narratives of belonging and community, allowing me to make meaningful relations between these private and public realms (Mills, 1959). Through analysing their narrative accounts I am able to explore the links between women's individual experiences and society (Riessman, 2000a; 2000b; Temple, 2001) and their constructions of intimacy with the world (Anthias, 2006), or the processes involved in how and to 'what' they feel and think they belong. Analysing narratives is also useful since narratives constitute past experience allowing people to make sense of the present (Riessman, 2008).

Focusing on women's narratives allows me to examine their reflexivity and how they anchor themselves in the world[5] (Sweetman, 2003) and how they exercise agency within the context of structural opportunities and constraints. Analysing women's narratives also provides an opportunity to explore their shifting ethnic, class, gendered and age-related positionalities, how these intersect − or translocate − and how they influence practices and outcomes. Analysing narratives is also useful when examining change and movement over time and space, since narrating allows the relationships between past, present and future and 'here' and 'there' to emerge (Bamberg, 2004). A structural narrative analytical methodology underpinned by an interpretivist epistemology provides rich in-depth information and a nuanced understanding of the 'qualitative significance of migration' (Halfacree, 2012, 211) for the women featured.

Narrative and plot

I see the plot of a narrative as the way by which events are coherently brought together (Czarniawska, 2004), how people organise such events and their experiences (Riessman, 1993; 2008), and also how narrative analysts impose structure (Ahmed, 2013). In any narrative, first there is a discrete succession or a series of incidents, and second, these incidents are configured into the story as a whole. In this way, people structure their experiences when they narrate, constructing one whole story out of multiple events (Ricoeur, 1984). This can be understood as emplotment: the creative centre of the narrative, or the poetic act (Ricoeur, 1984). Plots are linked to the social and cultural context of their production since all narratives are socially, temporally and culturally located and reflect and reproduce these locations (Ahmed, 2013). Examining the plot of a narrative allows for women's experiences of their material and social structural contexts to be explored and can be understood as 'narrative ethnography' (Holstein and Gubrium, 2000). It is also useful to analyse plot as women's thoughts, feelings, motives, agency, positionalities are illuminated. In this way, paying attention to plot gives insight into the 'practices' of women as agents in migration and the relationship between 'outcomes', mediated by positionalities within the context of wider structures.

Elsewhere (see Ahmed, 2013), I used the plot typologies the 'quest' and 'voyage and return' to make sense of women's divergent migration trajectories. I explained that women's narratives of 'lifestyle migration' are presented as a quest for a better life (Benson, 2011a) or if they return to the UK, as voyage and return. I developed the use of plot and argued that comparing the convergence and divergence of both plots allows for an understanding of retired women's lived experiences of migration, within the context of wider macro structures. I develop these ideas further throughout the book, relating plot to practices and outcomes in migration. An important feature of plot, is the 'the end point of plot movement' (Bakhtin, 1981, 89) or the ending embedded in the plot (Czarniawska, 2004), which is where the links between different events become apparent at the end. Women link their stories differently depending on the end point of plot movement (Bakhtin, 1981) in their narratives. The concept of 'narrative linkage' (Gubrium and Holstein, 2008) is also useful in relation to plot and understanding how the storyteller organises multiple incidents into a meaningful whole, since: 'No item of experience is meaningful in its own right. It is made meaningful through the particular ways it is linked to other items. Linkage creates a context for understanding' (Gubrium and Holstein, 2009, 55).

Narrative linkage also occurs when the narrator 'steps outside' the narrative to provide contextual detail or ethnographic understanding (Gubrium and Holstein, 2009). By analysing the convergence and divergence in the identified plots and differences in discursive strategies used, I examine how retired women living in Spain recount their experiences construct different positions (Ginsburg, 1989). Throughout my analysis I draw upon both aspects of narrative linkage, in relation to the plots of the 'quest' and 'voyage and return' and evolve this further by relating plot to practices and outcomes in retirement migration. I borrow the 'quest' and 'voyage and return' plot types from Christopher Booker's (2004) distillation of the seven basic plots from literature, film, the Bible, ancient myths and folk tales. Based on his interest on why people tell stories and the kinds of stories they tell, Booker (2004) typifies plots as: overcoming the monster; rags to riches; the quest; voyage and return; comedy; tragedy; and rebirth (Ahmed, 2013). A central figure characterises all plot types: for my purposes this is the women who narrate their experiences, and both the quest and voyage involve a journey, which for me, captures pre- and post-migration experiences, although the end points differ.

Stories based on the quest are predicated on the central character searching for something. Often this search is for a new home because something is wrong with the original one. For the women featured, the quest was for a new life and the recovery of something that had been lost: belonging and community. A 'call' triggers the quest and the central character feels an intense compulsion to leave the original home (Booker, 2004). Examining how women frame the call to migrate to Spain in retirement allows for an investigation of the multiple motivations in migration (Halfacree and Boyle, 1993), and this is addressed in Chapter Four. Regardless of whether the quest is a 'success', or if women voyage and return, the call is something that both plot typologies share. Divergence between the plots centres on whether the central character is able to achieve 'the life renewing goal' (Booker, 2004) or the quest's objective, which here is belonging and community in Spain. In order to fulfil this goal, women need to overcome certain obstacles (Oliver, 2008) and engage with quest companions (Booker, 2004). Throughout Chapters five to eight I disentangle women's post-migration practices in relation to belonging and community, focusing on place, networks and their shifting positionalities. Both typologies are useful to illuminate how women experience and construct 'home', representing fulfilment of the quest's goal of belonging and community. The main difference between these plots therefore, is the outcome: where the central character ultimately wants to be, in the original home in the UK, or the new one in Spain. Having considered the role of plot I now turn to focus on time.

Narrative and time

I have described plot above as bringing together disparate events into a coherent whole. Plot can also be understood as a work of composition, in terms of putting people's temporal experiences in order. In this way, within narrative, experiences are given meaning through the 'temporal dialectic' (Ricoeur, 1984; 1985; 1988) or the relating of time tenses, for example past, present and future which make life (and narrative) ordered. Time is a forgotten dimension in migration (Halfacree and Boyle, 1993 drawing on Shotter, 1984), and this is important since decisions to migrate are rooted in the context of people's lives: 'A specific migration exists as a part of our past, our present and our future; as part of our biography' (Halfacree and Boyle, 1993, 337). Analysing women's narratives in relation to time allows for a broader temporal perspective of their experiences of migration in relation to their biography, since people bring the past into the present through language, thus making sense of their lives (Riessman, 2008).

The narrated story is a temporal totality and the temporal identity of a story is something that endures and remains across that which passes and flows away (Ricoeur, 1984). Time as passage and duration, exemplified by past, present and future, characterises narratives. In this sense, we can see human experience as storied because we understand human actions as being organised in time (McAdams, 1993; Roberts, 2002). Composing a narrative therefore involves configuration and succession, and plot is linked to the time elements of the story which are selected, ordered and made meaningful within the account according to time. Temporal and spatial contexts are also epistemologically significant since: 'The narrator is located in time and space and the personal narrative emerges from a particular vantage point – the present; the stories we tell about the past always reflect our present concerns' (Day Sclater, 1998a, 75).

Talk of the past in narrative accounts is often used to explain or justify present actions and future intentions. However, as well as analytically bracketing aspects of structural analysis, within the remit of time and narrative I bracket further to examine a particular element of time, that is, the bringing of the past into the present in narrative through nostalgia: 'the assimilation of the past into the present' (Boym, 2001, 10). My analytical approach offers an opportunity to consider time in terms of how talking of the past influences the present and the future and particularly how nostalgia – the past in the present – imbues the accounts. Nostalgia (like community) can be something both real and imagined. The women I interviewed tended to tell a chronological story of their lives: often they would go back in time and provide an account of time passing up to the present as the following excerpt from Celia's narrative illustrates:

> 'Right, well; first of all, my thoughts. I'll go back to the beginning of when we first decided.' (Celia)

Analysing women's narratives is useful since they constitute past experience which allows them to make sense of the present (Riessman, 2008), and as Bakhtin (1981) explains:

> We somehow manage to endow all phenomena with meaning, that is, we incorporate them not only into the sphere of spatial and temporal existence, but also into a semantic sphere. (1981, 257)

Nostalgia as a chronotope

I have already suggested that nostalgia is important in discourses of community and it is now useful to highlight another way that nostalgia is significant in how it links time and space in narrative. Bakhtin (1981) in his critique of the Greek, Baroque and Gothic classical novel borrows the idea of the chronotope from Einstein's theory of relativity and reconceptualises it as 'a formally constitutive category of literature' (1981, 84) linking time and space together. For Bakhtin, the representational importance of the chronotope materialises in time and space:

> We will give the name *chronotope* (literally, 'time space') to the intrinsic connectedness of temporal and spatial relationships that are artistically expressed in literature…What counts for us is the fact that it expresses the inseparability of space and time. (Bakhtin, 1981, 84)

For me, the significance of chronotopes is their meaning for narrative, since: 'the chronotope is the place where the knots of narrative are tied and untied' (Bakhtin, 1981, 250). Although in migration, time–space compression (Harvey, 1989 cited in Torkington, 2012) means that all places are increasingly accessible, in narrative, through the chronotope, time and space are amplified, as Bakhtin suggests:

> In the literary artistic chronotope, spatial and temporal indicators are fused into one carefully thought-out, concrete whole. Time, as it were, thickens, takes on flesh, becomes artistically visible; likewise, space becomes charged and responsive to the movements of time, plot and history. (1981, 84)

Bakhtin (1981) identifies the adventure and idyllic chronotopes which link time and space together in literature in different ways. Adventure time, a feature of the classic Greek novel, takes place outside of biographical time and leaves no trace. To clarify, the beginning and end point of the plotline occur at separate times, in biographical time, but the events which occur within the these time frames have no particular chronology – adventure time does not unfold in biographical time – and events are not contingent on one another:

> The adventure chronotope is thus characterised by a technical abstract connection between space and time by the reversibility of moments in a temporal sequence, and by the interchangeability of space. (Bakhtin, 1981, 100)

In this way, the adventure chronotope, or adventure time, is characterised by 'random temporal contingencies' (Skultans, 1997, 86) and emerges at the point of rupture in real life (Bakhtin, 1981): unusual or noteworthy events occur and shape the protagonist. It is the adventure time of everyday life which I find useful to analyse women's experiences of migration in retirement, particularly in relation to the call at the start of the quest. Like classic adventure time, the adventure time of everyday life occurs at times of biographical disruption, creating a new chronotope, and this is a mix of adventure time and everyday time. In other words, 'a special sort of everyday time' (Bakhtin, 1981, 111). Every day adventure time represents:

> A time of exceptional and unusual events, events determined by chance, which moreover, manifest themselves in fortuitous encounters. (Bakhtin, 1981: 116)

According to Bakhtin (1981), the initial and final links in everyday adventure time lie beyond the power of chance, and this also provides a route to analysing of women's agency and practices within the context of wider social structures. Everyday adventure time is useful in analysing biological disruption in women's narratives in conjunction with their narrative footing and positionalities since it illuminates the contexts in which they live and provides access to how they see themselves in such contexts.

A further chronotope, the idyllic chronotope – or folkloric time – also links time and space. Unlike adventure time, idyllic time is rooted to the earth and the physical environment, there is conjoining of human life with nature and blurring of temporal boundaries, representing:

> An organic fastening down, a grafting of life and its events to a place, to a familiar territory. (Bakhtin, 1981, 225)

I suggest that nostalgia – underpinning a motif of loss, in this case of community and belonging – is chronotopic since it links a lost place and also a lost time through narrative. The past is recalled to reconcile our identities in the present (Riessman 2008), and, a 'Focus on the past is particularly important as a structuring device' (Skultans, 1998, 85).[6]

Just as Skultans (1998) describes Latvian forests as physical and moral refuges or 'the pastoral idyll', I consider women's narratives of community in Spain as a refuge or Mediterranean idyll, and also explore how the UK is reconfigured if the quest is not successful. These ideas will be used in relation to how women superimpose their desires and wants onto place and how nostalgic recollections across time/space are constructed through narratives. The quest's goal for a new home or a place of safety (adventure and idyll), and how nostalgic recollections are linked to both space and time will be investigated. I particularly focus on how plot (quest and voyage and return) are linked to notions of the idyll and explore the inter-relatedness of adventure and idyllic time in women's narratives, developing the idea of nostalgia as a chronotope. Places when imbued with idyllic properties can be seen as being suspended in time but brought into the present through nostalgia in narrative. I now discuss how narrative illuminates women's positionalities and how they construct identities.

Narrative, identity and positionality

The term identity is often used a fixed way of attempting to understand who one feels and thinks one is and does not allow for any consideration of the processes which lead to identity formation, or the context in which identities are constructed and performed. Anthias (2002) argues that although identity has analytical value, using the concept 'obscures, reintroducing essentialism through the back door' (2002, 492). However, within an interpretivist epistemological perspective – and in many other narrative uses of identity (for example Holstein and Gubrium, 2000; Riessman, 1990b; 2000a; 2000b; Temple, 2008a) – 'identity' is not presented as being fixed or having an essence. I do not see women as inhabiting the social categories or identities highlighted above, or that these are predetermined; instead, they are fluid and situated and I focus on the processes involved in constructing them.

There are multiple 'locations' and contexts from which belongings are imagined and constructed. These locations can be understood as 'translocations' in terms of a range of social positions, social divisions and identities (Anthias, 2008) and these overlap. Attempts to understand how social positions overlap have previously been framed in terms of intersectionality (Crenshaw, 1989; Fuss, 1989) which can be understood as the interconnectedness between social divisions (Anthias, 2008), the relationship between different social categories (Valentine, 2007) or the 'interlocking categories of experience' (Anderson and Hill Collins, 1992, xii). Intersectionality was previously used by critical race theorists and black feminists to understand the position of black women in terms of multiple and reinforcing types of oppression (Staunæs, 2010). It 'captures the recognition that difference is located not in the spaces between identities but within' (Crenshaw et al, 1995, 12). Intersections of different categories are not stable, people's identity is not fixed, and there is constant movement between subject positions which are influenced by context. However, intersectionality, although useful, is a rather rigid and mechanistic way of conceptualising how multiple and overlapping identities (or positionalities) relate to one another, since it does not allow for a consideration of the processes and practices involved in identity construction, or for the impact on structures and individuals (Anthias, 2008). It is difficult to research intersectionality (Crenshaw et al, 1995), although examining the everyday lives of subjects to unravel how different positions are experienced is a good place to begin (McCall, 2005). I explain below how narrative analysis facilitates this.

From the discussion here, it will be becoming evident that narrative identity is continuous over time and changes according to context (Ricoeur, 1988; Temple, 2008a). Narrative identity also illuminates the contexts in which people are located and how they see themselves in such contexts. Through narrating we present and construct our identities (Temple, 2008a; Ahmed, 2011): identity is strategic and positional, rather than essentialist (Hall, 2000) and narratives do not reveal who we are (Temple, 2008a). Identity is conceptually important in offering explanations of social and cultural change in terms of which identities people feel and choose to belong to (Woodward, 2002; du Gay et al, 2000; Temple, 2008a). Narrative identity can be understood to be about similarity and difference – denoting boundaries – and it can be multiple and is also relational. Somers (1994) uses 'positioning' to describe how the narrator establishes her identity through narrative practice in relation to the listener and how this also constructs the identity of the researcher. Gubrium and Holstein (1998) refer to this process of shifting positionalities as 'narrative footing', so the focus is on the identity that the narrator 'performs' through the narrative act (Riessman, 1993; 2000a; Goffman, 1959; 1975; 1981). Another way of looking at this is in terms of how participants negotiate how they want to be known by the stories they develop with their audience (Riessman, 2000b) and how they in turn choose to cast the audience or how narrators set up subject positions (Day Sclater, 1998a). This all affects the research process and how the story is told, as I discuss throughout the following chapter.

Women's 'identities' can therefore be understood as the construction and presentation of their subjective experiences through their narratives. The focus on performance is useful to understand how people represent their lives (see Roberts, 2008), and in this way, analysing performance is useful in examining how women as narrators perform their multiple and shifting identities within their accounts. Gubrium and Holstein (1998) refer to this as 'narrative slippage', or a way of thinking about the self in relation to others and how this changes as expressed through narratives. Day Sclater refers to such apparent contradictions, when a narrator can revisit old themes (and I also suggest subject positions) and speak of them differently as 'transformation of subjectivity' (1998a: 67).

Both participants and researchers portray themselves as located within their accounts in particular ways. Any narrative identity is inscribed with social characteristics since:

> People present themselves differently in different settings and the 'same act' can have different meanings. (Temple, 2001, 71)

Narratives of location then, can be understood as accounts of the processes of identity construction and as the context in which these processes operate; or how we locate ourselves in terms of the many categories that are socially available to us, for example class, ethnicity, gender, age. Therefore, using translocational positionality (Anthias, 2002) has epistemological value since it is concerned with performance and process (Holstein and Gubrium, 2000). Focusing on the performative or dialogic in narrative adds a further analytical dimension (Riessman, 2008; Roberts, 2008) – looking at 'whom' the narrative is for and how it is a joint production between the narrator and the audience.[7] I explore how women locate themselves in terms of their positionalities and examine identity in narrative in a way that focuses on context, meaning and practice, and how identity is constructed in and through narrative. I examine interaction in terms of how women as narrators position other characters in their narratives and sometimes me – as the researcher. Considering the positionalities that women present through their narratives allows for an examination of the construction of multiple, complex and shifting belongings across space and time.

Significantly, narratives are often moral tales and Riessman (2003; 2008), drawing on Goffman's (1959) dramaturgical metaphor, argues that 'social actors stage performances of desirable selves to preserve "face" in situations of difficulty' (Riessman, 2003, 7). May (2008), also influenced by Goffman (1959) refers to moral or acceptable 'selfs' which are '[s]ignposts to what the governing norms of a society are, how these are negotiated in particular social situations that present a moral dilemma' (2008, 470). For these women, choosing to move abroad in retirement presents several moral dilemmas or obstacles to overcome as I discuss throughout Chapters Five to Nine.

Conducting the research

I met all of the women I interviewed in numerous social situations over a 12-month period before engaging them in the research. I am not claiming that my sample is representative of all retired migrants from the UK in Spain; indeed, to attempt this would have been futile since no sampling frame was available. Rather, my purpose was to capture the experiences of women from the UK who had retired and moved to

Spain, both permanently and part time, with partners and alone. When I embarked on the research I aimed to interview around 20 women. However, I stopped at 17 as I felt theoretical saturation had been reached and that I had sufficient data for meaningful structural narrative analysis. I stopped interviewing when accounts became repetitive despite differences in the biographies of participants (Sherlock, 2002) and the analytical categories became clear. I conducted one narrative interview with each of the women; interviews lasted between an hour and 45 minutes and just over three hours. I began each interview with a 'grand tour question' (Spradley, 1979), asking the women to tell me about themselves and how they came to be in Spain. Fifteen of the interviews took place in the women's homes, while the remaining two took place in a friend's house. Although the sample size is small, using a structural as well as thematic narrative approach yields rich description (Riessman, 2005).

Analysing narratives

In practical terms, I analysed women's narratives in three related ways (Riessman, 2008). First I looked at the content, in other words *what* was said.[8] This involved examining the themes arising from the data (and interpretive decisions shaped the focus here) which allowed for categorical exploration within as well as across cases referring to prior theory. Because of its focus on content, the context in which data are generated and the reflexive role of the researcher (Charmaz, 1995), thematic narrative analysis is sometimes confused with grounded theory. However, grounded theory does not take account of language, structure and performance (Riessman, 1993; 2008; Ahmed, 2013), although I share with its proponents a view of qualitative research being more than intuitive and superficial and a precursor to 'real' quantitative data generation (Charmaz, 1983, 1995; Glaser and Strauss, 1967).

Second, I looked at *how* women told their stories, in other words at the ways the narratives were constructed to persuade me (the researcher) of their plausibility. Researchers need to be mindful that observations of people's actions do not necessarily tally with what people say that they do (Crow and Mah, 2012), and I acknowledge that women's narratives are subjective accounts, influenced by context; any knowledge that is generated has to take this and the women's previous experiences into account. Further, my understanding is necessarily shaped by my subjective positionalities and experiences which are also both multiple and non-measurable: I cannot edit myself out.[9] Ricoeur (1984) refers to narrative understanding rather than truth as such, and I analyse the coherence and persuasiveness (Hatch and Wismiewski, 1995) of women's narrative accounts, by looking at linguistic devices employed, narrative plot and time, illuminating the contexts in which women's lives are lived and how they present their class, gendered, ethnic and age-related positionalities.

My approach to examining language has been influenced by Derrida (1967) and deconstruction[10] and I draw on Czarniawska (2004) to analyse the use of the following linguistic devices which attempt to persuade the audience: apologia, which represents a defence, actual or potential against accusation; eulogy, a speech filled with praise or commendation; hyperbole, the use of exaggerated terms for emphasis; hypothyposis, a visually powerful and vivid description; irony or inverted meaning; and mimesis which is the imitation of another's words. Finally, I addressed the '*who*' of the narratives or how talk was shaped and performed by the teller's shifting positionalities (Anthias, 2002) or identity.

I also consider women's narratives as 'counter-narratives' (Andrews and Bamberg, 2004) to government meta-narratives of community both in terms of its positive and negative connotations (Mooney and Neal, 2008) to further understand their experiences of belonging and non-belonging in Spain.

In qualitative research the relationship between the sample and the wider population is not always based on demographic representation (Mason, 2002). There is, however, an issue concerning how I can make claims from the sample I have chosen since the findings represent a temporal and cultural context. While the sample in this qualitative inquiry is small, women were selected purposively for the contribution that they can make to theory, and theory from this study in Spain may be used to illuminate other experiences of retirement migration in new situations (Morse, 1999), and to highlight how the processes of constructing belonging and identity-making practices are changing and becoming more complex for retired migrant women. Moreover, such theory can contribute to knowledge development when it is recontextualised in numerous different settings, amounting to theory based generalisation (Morse, 1994). Therefore, if emerging knowledge about narrative constructions of belonging and community accurately describe and explain phenomena in other situations, then these ideas could be theoretically generalisable. Throughout my analysis I will demonstrate that although the women's stories were unique and personal, their subjective truths have wider resonance (Day Sclater, 1998a).

Conclusion

Above, I discussed my approach to gaining knowledge of community and belonging in retirement migration. I use the term 'retirement migration' to categorise women's migration to Spain, but I do not present retirement migration as a simple typology which explains women's experiences. Instead, women's migratory decisions are located in their biographies which I explore through a structural narrative analytical framework, and use this to illuminate the structures, practices and outcomes of women as agents with multiple and shifting positionalities. I explained that nostalgia as a chronotope is useful to understand retired women's experiences of belonging and community in migration since it links time and space in narrative. In the following chapter I examine in more detail the structures and positionalities of the women featured: in other words I focus on the contexts in which their migration takes place and also on their age, gendered, ethnic and class-related social locations.

THREE

Locating the women:
macro, meso and micro contexts

Introduction

In the previous chapter I explained my approach to gaining knowledge of the processes involved in constructing shifting and overlapping forms of belonging to different kinds of community. I argued that a thematic and structural narrative approach can illuminate how retired women experience the structural contexts in which their migration takes place, how this shapes agency,[1] and how structures and agency are mediated by their multiple and shifting positionalities. In this chapter I discuss the macro contexts framing retired women's agency in migration in terms of 'upper structural layers' and 'more proximate structural layers' (O'Reilly, 2012). The focus then shifts to the women's positionalities, and I explore how positionalities act as a meso level of interaction between wider structures and women's agency. I develop my use of translocational positionality and discuss this in relation to gender, class, age and ethnicity and place this in theoretical and lived contexts. I also offer a reflection on my own positionalities.

Structural contexts in retirement migration

In the introduction, I summarised the reasons for the rise in retirement migration in Europe. Now, it is useful to revisit this discussion in order to explain British working-class women's experiences in terms of the structural, demographic and cultural contexts framing their migratory decisions. It is worth noting that in retirement/lifestyle migration, the structural context tends to represent opportunities rather than constraints (O'Reilly, 2012). The temporal context in which women's retirement migration took place is also significant; they moved in the late 1990s and early 2000s, before the global recession, when the pound was strong against the peseta.[2] In 2003–04, when the fieldwork was conducted, the cost of living in Spain was approximately two-thirds of what it was in the UK and the exchange rate favoured sterling as one euro was equivalent to 60 pence.[3] All of the women featured mentioned the differences between the cost of living in the UK and Spain as a factor influencing their migration to Spain as Margot's talk about her financial difficulties in the UK illustrates:

> 'I was finding it very difficult to manage financially...I had the bailiffs come round to take my stuff away...I'd over run the council tax bill.' (Margot)

Myra equates retirement in the UK as 'existing' whereas in Spain she has a 'life'

> 'I mean managing an old age pension in England just you're just barely existing, where out here you've got a life. It's plenty out here.' (Myra)

These women had all previously been to the Costa Blanca on holiday and this influenced their decision to move there in retirement as suggested by the excerpts from Celia and Cynthia's narratives:

> 'Me and my husband have been to Spain loads of times over the years and I always wanted to stay here.' (Celia)

> 'Well, how I came to be in Spain...for years I've visited Spain on holiday.' (Cynthia)

Women's experiences of mass tourism (as an 'upper layer' external structure) also influenced their decision to move in retirement in terms of shaping their aspirations. The 1992 Maastricht Treaty and EU enlargement, allowing freedom of movement also represent upper structural layers – as do globalisation and increases in technology. These upper structural layers, combined with more proximate structural layers (O'Reilly, 2012), for example, speculative development, house building and the marketing of properties by agents to a British market, all intersect with retirement which represents a further opportunity facilitating migration and a lack of constraint (from being tied to employment).

Demographic and cultural contexts as structures are also important in understanding retirement migration for these women, who can be described as belonging to the demographic group the 'baby boomers'. This generation is often associated with increased opportunities, growing up in a time of post-war affluence and being in good health.[4]

The term is also sometimes associated with the rejection of traditional values and this generation is characterised by a mass consumer revolution, increases in affluence, capital gains from owner-occupation and the opportunity to retire early (Ahmed, 2011). Baby boomers were also the first generation to experience foreign travel and cheap air fares and, arguably, able to make different choices from previous generations in terms of quality of life considerations and attitudes towards caring roles (Phillipson et al, 2008). In this way, retirement migration can also be understood in terms of increased individualisation (Beck, 1992) and freedom from constraints, which is significant for these women since this has resulted in changes in traditional family relations. In Northern Europe, cultural expectations – as well as laws and social policies – shape perceptions of obligation and responsibility towards family members (Herlofson and Hagestad, 2012). These structural contexts further enable (rather than constrain) the women featured in terms of their migratory decisions. In this way, women are no longer identifying themselves primarily in terms of family or care-giving roles (Guberman et al, 2011). Geographical distance and changes in role expectations are therefore significant in understanding how more proximate structural layers facilitate women's movement abroad in retirement.

Since globalisation is encouraging increased mobility of families and other changes in intergenerational relationships (Lowenstein et al, 2011), contemporary grandmothering is usefully considered within the context of international retirement migration. Traditionally, studies of intergenerational relationships have largely been concerned with factors influencing the frequency and quality of contact and how these affect care-giving roles and responsibilities and finance transfers (Ko, 2012). Research focused on grandparenting has privileged the centrality of grandmothers and their kinship keeping role (Herlofson and Hageststad, 2012), while studies of younger generations have examined mobility and how this affects their lives (Brannen, 2003). However, new forms of grandmothering are emerging as a result of international retirement migration, and it is therefore timely to explore how such new forms of grandmothering are experienced and constructed. It is also important to consider how older women exercise and experience mobility and how this creates a divergent lifestyle (Brannen, 2003) from traditional expectations of the grandmother role. I explore this in detail in Chapter Eight.

So while there is recognition that that people move to Spain in retirement because of a wide range of structural, demographic and cultural shifts in society, these alone cannot explain individual agency. Although women's decision to move to Spain was made within such contexts, to fully understand their actions, attention must be paid to how they experience them. Upper structural layers, including increased global movement, mass tourism and EU enlargement, and more proximate structural layers, for example retirement, the development and marketing of properties in Spain, affordable and frequent air transport and changes in western cultural expectations of grandmothers all shape women's agency. How structures are experienced and how they enable and constrain agency is also mediated by women's social field (Levitt and Glick Schiller, 2004) which includes their class position and their dispositions and view of the world, gender and generation (Van Hear, 2010) and ethnicity; or as I have previously termed this, positionalites which represent a meso[5] level between structure and agency.[6] The interdependence of structures, agency and positionalities influences 'practices' or the way women live in the world – and also influences outcomes, or what happens and how they experience and construct belonging and community in Spain in retirement.

Positionalities in retirement migration

I have suggested that using positionality is a less fixed way of understanding the multiple, overlapping and shifting identities that people construct and are ascribed. To recapitulate, positionality can be understood as the ways in which social divisions – or categories, 'social ontologies around different material processes in social life' (Anthias, 2008, 13) – inter-relate in terms of producing social relations. Social positioning relates to the practices, outcomes and processes involved in constructing multiple identities. These categories also exist in the imaginary realm, and are constructed, and people may find themselves assigned different positions depending on context and on their own understanding of 'who' they are, when, where and how. It is not possible to wholly explain retired women's experiences of belonging and community in migration through a single framework or one social category; instead their multiple positionalities or locations must be taken into account. Positionality can be understood in terms of social position, or as an outcome of social processes and also in relation to social positioning, which relates to the processes in constructing positionality (Anthias, 2008; Didero, 2011). In summary, a focus on positionality is a useful tool to understand the meso level between structure and agency since it allows for a consideration of the processes involved in identity construction, taking account of agency framed by wider social structures. This analysis is continued throughout the book as women's journeys unfold. I now begin to discuss women's multiple positionalities in relation to gender, class, age and ethnicity.

Gender

Although I focus on gender as a positionality, I acknowledge women's bodily inscription (and ascription) and material reality: 'woman' is a socially and politically constructed category, the ontological basis of which lies in a set of experiences rooted in the material world (Stanley and Wise, 1990, 21). Gender can also be understood in terms of social differentiation and social relations (Anthias et al, 2012), or 'constructed power relations that are embedded in social processes and institutionalised in ways that have consequences for life choices across the life course' (McDonald, 2011, 1187). However, gender does not transcend all other social locations (King, 2012a) and women do not constitute a homogeneous group: there are divisions within gender.

Women have a range of locations within gender, and gender is situational and translocates with other positions within wider structural contexts. In the introduction I highlighted the different groupings of the women in terms of whether they moved to Spain alone, with husbands or partners and these different locations also need to be taken into account. My focus on gender takes account of its fluidity (Ryan and Webster, 2008) and relates to women's experiences of retirement migration in terms of how gender shapes their experiences of migration; gendered dynamics within the household regarding agency, influence and decision making; the kinds of networks women construct and belong to and how they renegotiate family responsibilities from a distance, particularly with grandchildren.

Age

Traditionally, ageing was equated with the opposite of mobility, but now there are different representations of ageing, and migration can be seen as a way to counter the negative aspects of getter older (Oliver, 2008; Nilsson, 2013). Theories in social gerontology and migration have predominantly focused on disadvantaged minority ethnic groups (McDonald, 2011), although King et al (2000); Huber and O'Reilly (2004); Oliver (2008); and Benson (2011a, 2011b) capture the experiences of mainly affluent retired migrants from the UK. King et al's (2000) and Oliver's (2008) study of migration to the Algarve, Tuscany and Malta and the Costa del Sol (King et al, 2000; Oliver, 2008) focus on new constructions of old age and positive ageing, and how retirees negotiate freedom in new contexts. Theories of successful (or positive) ageing relate to how older adults enhance their lives and centre on how people exercise agency and choice. They can also be understood as a reworking of classical activity theory, or how older people maintain independence in later life (McDonald, 2011). My focus is not so much on ageing as a category of experience as in Oliver's 2008 study, or on positive ageing, but rather on how retirement represents opportunities and shapes migration from an age-related vantage point which translocates with other positionalities. A second set of theories to explain adjustments to ageing can be typified as 'disengagement theories', relating to how people withdraw from society as they age (McDonald, 2011; and see Rowe and Kahn, 1997). Again, I am not explicitly using these theories but draw from the idea of disengagement in terms of how women disentangle themselves from their lives in the UK, and the UK itself. A third set of gerontology theories I acknowledge, can be understood as continuity theories (McDonald, 2011) which relate to how people hold on to parts of their past as they age. This aspect is important to my understanding of retired British women's experiences in Spain: for them it is an imagined past. Choosing to move to Spain in retirement could be read as moving back in time, and they attempt to create what is familiar, or: 'the same somewhere else' (Nilsson, 2013). It is worth noting, that with the exception of Mable, aged 83; Phyllis, aged 77, and Agnes, aged 69, most of the women were relatively young older people, in their "third age'.[7] As Cynthia indicates:

'Well I'm only 54, so I suppose that's young for retiring.' (Cynthia)

Ethnicity

Ethnic categories can be understood as forms of social organisation, with boundaries denoting who belongs (Anthias, 2002), and who does not. I have already mentioned that belonging to groups or places often encompasses a feeling or sense of something, and, similarly, ethnic affiliation can be imagined. I see ethnicity as a construction based on country of origin, an identification and identifier, or as a social position which has contextual meaning. Skey's (2011) discussion of the different dimensions of national discourse is useful in relation to understanding the relationship between national belonging and ethnic identity. He outlines five dimensions as follows: first, the concept of territory underpins national conceptions and imaginations related to space;

second, there are temporal dimensions since the past is articulated in national terms; third, cultural dimensions or norms shape national (and ethnic) belonging; fourth, political dimensions; and fifth, the self/other which denotes people and values. Women's ethnic positionalities are shaped by being from the UK and also by being in Spain. Importantly, their ethnic positionalities are also relational: people become more sensitive to their own culture when they encounter others (Cohen, 1985). However, not all women recognise that they have an ethnicity as such; for example, Cynthia ascribes ethnicity to others, but not to herself, suggesting that 'whiteness is so deeply entrenched as "the norm" that white people fail to recognise that they have an ethnicity' (Bonnett, 2000):

'I have friends who are of ethnic origin.' (Cynthia)

Class

As indicated earlier, people choose migration destinations congruent with their lifestyle preferences and biographies (Conway, 2003). Previous studies of retirement migration have tended to focus on the motivations and experiences of more affluent migrants (King et al, 2000), and how such class positions are reproduced through practising culture in migration (Oliver and O'Reilly, 2010; Benson, 2011a; 2011b). Lifestyle migrants are often middle-class migrants with high levels of social and cultural capital (Salazar, 2014). Significantly, the majority of the women in my study were not particularly affluent, only Lillian and Joy described themselves as being well-off, and can be described as 'working class' – although nobody used the term 'class' – and few were educated beyond secondary school. However, people tend not to articulate their identities in terms of class, and often class identity is weak, but this does not mean that class is unimportant (Savage, Bagnall and Longhurst, 2001). Savage et al (2001) describe class as a social identity and argue that there is an 'impasse' in terms of class analysis since it is difficult to define and problematic to study. However, they argue that although class identities are 'ambivalent and weak', it is still possible to analyse class. This approach is useful, since I share with Savage et al (2001) an interest in how class identity – or positionality – can be understood and particularly how it shapes retired women's experiences of migration to Spain.

For Bourdieu (1977), in exploring how social class is practised, the key concepts are social field and habitus: social field refers to both social space and the interactions which take place. A person's (or group) habitus reproduces social field and people feel comfortable with others whom they perceive to be like them. I am using positionalities in a similar way to habitus, in that it mediates between structure and agency, but I argue that positionality is useful for my analysis since it also allows for account to be taken of the fluidity and shifts in position, and for an examination of the processes involved in translocation. People see their own class (habitus) as 'the norm' (Bourdieu, 1977) and this also allows them to categorise other people: that's not for the likes of us' (Bourdieu, 1977, 77). The excerpt from Lillian's narrative below illustrates how cultural distinction is drawn to express identity, although class is not explicitly referred to:

> 'I don't go there [to the Silver Ladies club]. It's not me you see.' (Lillian)

However, whichever class people identify with, is seen by them as 'ordinary' (Savage et al, 2001). Lillian does not present her discernment as unusual, but as natural and 'normal' by saying:

> 'We're only friends with normal people.' (Lillian)

Ordinariness for the women in this study is key, and relates to them not positioning themselves as privileged or wealthy in the main, as Celia and Cynthia emphasise:

> 'Although people have this image of pensioners now being wealthy, and they think that just because you've moved to Spain, people's philosophy is, "Oh, you've got a house in Spain you must be rich." But what they forget is that we've had to sell our homes in England to do this, and we're having to look after ourselves here, so we're not wealthy.' (Cynthia)

> 'Another reason we decided to come here permanently; first of all we thought we'd have it as a holiday home – and probably sell our house and buy a little flat – so we could go backwards and forwards...but we're not wealthy people. So to have to keep two homes running, we thought maybe we should just go and do it.' (Celia)

Instead, women cast themselves as hardworking and deserving their life in Spain. However, although class is more than occupation, people's sense of worth, or identity is often tied up with their work. Being 'working class' does not have to be stigmatised as a class identity, instead it can be seen as a moral force (Skeggs, 1997) and this was apparent for a number of women in this study who used previous employment as narrative footing in several key ways; to contextualise their lives before migration and also to justify exercising individualism, as Cynthia demonstrates:

> 'I did two jobs, so I worked Monday to Friday as a parts manager for a diesel engine company and then I worked weekends selling houses in Spain. Well not actually selling…I was promoting houses.' (Cynthia)

Celia and Cynthia talk about their pre-migration lives and how they managed working and the domestic duties associated with being a wife and mother. They portray a life of resigned monotony and here class and gender translocate:

> 'You get up early, you make the bed, you wash the pots, you go to work …You come home from work, you do your jobs. You're ready for bed aren't you?' (Celia)

> 'Certainly for the last 20 years in Britain mainly because women have gone out to work…everybody's working and when they get home from work, it's coats off, cook the tea and then ready for bed.' (Cynthia)

Both Mabel and Bernice begin by stating their age and previous occupation. Mabel's narrative footing captures the translocation of age, gender and class and also illuminates the cultural and temporal contexts of her life:

> 'I'm 83 years old. I'm a retired teacher, head teacher. I'm a science graduate from [Oxbridge]…I was a London teacher, I loved Cockney kids and I loved, you know, teaching in a big school…Really highly qualified women…used to have to go into teaching. There wasn't very much else…I worked for [a travel agent] during the long school holidays, because I lived in an era when women teachers had unequal pay and I had a son…I was married to a Frenchman and after the war we didn't hit it off and he went back to France and I was a single parent before they were invented.' (Mabel)

Mabel was the oldest woman who participated in my study and came from a more privileged background than the others. However, she was keen to play down the cultural distinction between herself and her compatriots, and her identification with 'Cockney kids' is the first clue to this. In spite of her background and Oxbridge education, Mabel's life was circumscribed by her gendered positionality; having to go into teaching as there were no other career options for educated women, being a single parent in the 1950s and having to take a second job to support herself and her son as her teaching salary was less than that of her male counterparts.

Bernice talked about her long and hard working life with pride. Additional satisfaction was conveyed through her talk of her paid work not compromising her responsibilities towards her children, and there is evidence of Berenice's class position as a 'moral force' (Skeggs, 1997) at work. The meshing of age, class and gendered positionalities are also differently apparent here:

> 'I'm 63 this month, I worked until I was nearly 61 and worked most of my life…I've done all sorts of jobs, I've never, you know, once I'd been back to work after I'd had the children I didn't…whatever I've done I've taken a job, even though it was a horrible job…but I never left my children with anybody else. I stayed at home with them [until] they were school age and my jobs were part time. I took any job just to keep working.' (Bernice)

For Bernice, being a good mother was about putting her children first and being their primary carer, and she managed to achieve this while working. There is a subtext in Bernice's narrative, a recognition of expectations of what represents a 'good mother' to fulfil this particular gender role. This was also apparent in Lillian's narrative, although her circumstances differed:

> 'I didn't go to work while I had the children, I was lucky I didn't have to…my husband worked very, very hard for a long time and the boys always had everything they needed…We always had lovely holidays, lovely homes and we maintained that for 40 years.' (Lillian)

Not untypically, Lillian had a traditional view of paid employment regarding women of her generation with children; she saw it as a necessary supplement to the household's finances, if the 'husband' was unable to provide. She described herself as 'lucky', in that she was able to prioritise her children when they were young, but like Brenda, when her children were older, she willingly returned to part-time work:

'I worked for Marks and Spencer counting money.' (Lillian)

Lillian acknowledged her relative privilege but emphasised that their lives had not always been affluent and that it was important to adapt to changes in circumstances. In this way she conveyed a strong sense of working hard and not taking prosperity for granted:

'Life doesn't remain the same; you have to keep phases in your life, whatever you're doing at the time, how old your children are, whether you're working, whether you're not because your husband's doing well at work, if he's not you cut your cloth accordingly…We've always stretched ourselves, when we've wanted to do something we've done it. If we've wanted to buy a house with a big swimming pool, tennis courts we did it, you know.' (Lillian)

Joy had never been in paid employment, and defined herself in relation to her domestic roles to contextualise her life before migration:

'I was a full-time wife, mother and housekeeper.' (Joy)

Joy was quite matter of fact about her circumstances. Her husband had previously had a very well-paid job and she did not need to work. Her husband who was 20 years older than her had been retired for over 20 years, since Joy was 34:

'Well we haven't had any money worries, so certainly when we left the house in Surrey…we embarked upon lots of holidays; we had cruises and trips here there and everywhere.' (Joy)

Once Joy's twin boys left home, she found herself with another domestic role to fulfil:

'My husband retired 20 years ago now…and became a full-time sort of slouch; down the pub when it opened, sleep the afternoon, you know. He didn't do anything really very much and to an extent I suppose I've been his full-time carer for a number of years.' (Joy)

Deidre presents a number of positionalities in the following extract from the start of her narrative:

'My name is Deidre Helmshore, I was a librarian at [a] university. Previous to that I was a stepmother to three boys and I lived in [the north-west of England]. Before that I was in South America for six years. My first husband was an accountant, he saw an advert in the newspaper for accountants back in the Andes in Peru and we both fancied travelling…My second husband was a university lecturer, a widow and he had these three young boys and I looked after them. I had a very good upbringing, good childhood, quite family orientated and basically that's how I see myself. And also I'm gay.' (Deirdre)

Deidre provides narrative footing by providing her credentials. She worked at the library when she left her second husband and moved to Yorkshire to be with Vera. She casts herself as family orientated, having had a good upbringing herself and also by her role as stepmother to her husband's children. She also positions herself as a woman of the world, an adventuress having lived in South America with her first husband. Mentioning that she is gay on first reading seems almost an afterthought. I am not ignoring the fact that Deirdre and Vera are gay, but I am not analysing this as a positionality, although recognise that this is another important social location which has not received as much attention as gender and race (Brown, 2012). I also acknowledge that in addition to being historically gender blind, migration research has also been characterised by heteronormative assumptions (Manalansan, 2006). This is the only time that Deirdre refers to her sexuality throughout the course of her narrative, and Vera did not mention this at all. In terms of their lives in Spain they were 'out' as a couple, they socialised with other (heterosexual) couples and also engaged in women only social fields, for example the Silver Ladies club.

However, Deidre was 'known' to me, I had been friends with her and Vera[8] for over ten years by the time they moved to Spain, so I already knew this. Looking more closely at the text and Deidre's positionings, sheds light on the cultural and material circumstances of her life. When Deidre was a young woman in the late 1950s and early 1960s it would have been less acceptable to live a 'non-heterosexual' life, and her financial dependence on both husbands reflects the temporal context in which her positionalities were framed.

Like Deirdre, Vera establishes her credentials in terms of employment history which serves to contextualise the desire for an improved quality of life in retirement:

> 'I'm nearly 60 years of age. I've had quite a varied life in terms of employment, worked mainly in offices, had my own business for 10 years, then went to university, was a very mature student worked in [local government] which I enjoyed but then took a sideways move into [the voluntary sector].' (Vera)

As I have already suggested, it is not possible to properly explicate retired women's experiences of migration, and how they construct belonging and community through the lens of one social category. Their numerous, overlapping and shifting social locations need to be explored and I begin to do this above. The influence of positionalities on women's agency is further explored throughout the following chapters. Now though, it is necessary for me to reflect on my own positionalities.

Reflexivity: locating myself in the research

I include a discussion of my location in the research for two related reasons; first, to be transparent by documenting the data generation process (Riessman, 2008), and second, to locate myself in terms of my translocational positionalities, that is, the processes and outcomes of my position in the social order and my views on where I belong (Anthias, 2002; Anthias and Cederberg, 2009). The development and application of reflexivity in social inquiry has gathered momentum as a result of the emergence of the linguistic or interpretive turn and feminist research. In examining my position, the concept 'reflexivity' is useful in acknowledging the role that the researcher plays in shaping knowledge generated since the interview is not just a 'reality report' – in line with my epistemology – but rather presents an opportunity for constructing identities through narrative for both participants and researcher (Harding, 2006). Further, a narrative approach is useful in addressing the relationship between the researcher and their reflexive role (Colombo, 2003).

The term 'self-reflexive personal' (Grace et al, 2006) can also be understood as a range of identity positions which are not necessarily chosen by the researcher and can change throughout the course of the interview (Ladino, 2002). However, although it is important for me to examine and highlight my multiple social locations, I acknowledge that it is impossible to measure how these affected my practice as a researcher and how I influenced the data generated.

Just as knowledge is contextually specific, the researcher's assumed and assigned subjectivity – or identity – is also significant in terms of the knowledge produced, since: 'Researchers' understandings are necessarily temporally, intellectually, politically and emotionally grounded and are thus as contextually specific as those of "the researched"' (Stanley and Wise, 1990, 23). The interview is a collaboration and the 'position' of the researcher and subjective and intersubjective elements need to be taken into account in order that researchers can claim integrity and trustworthiness (Finlay, 2002).

Even being an 'insider' or sharing social locations with research participants does not over-ride differences and create 'insiderness' (Merton,1972). Further, being perceived as an 'insider' can generate different kinds of barriers: there can be an over-conformity to cultural norms and being an outsider can allow for further insights to be gained as it would not be assumed that researchers have predetermined knowledge (Windance Twine and Warren, 2000). Assumptions about the status of insiderness and outsiderness are foundationalist and essentialist (Rhodes, 1996; Windance Twine and Warren, 2000) since people have multiple identifications (Windance Twine and Warren, 2000). Any common ground and divergence is to a large extent perceived, and it is an interpretive choice in terms of how it is seen to have an impact on the data produced. I have multiple positionalities and some might be considered 'insider'. It is a partial condition which shifts throughout the course of the interview. Moreover, there are dilemmas in both being an insider (known) while being an obvious outsider (a stranger) (Perez, 2006).

It is also worth acknowledging that attempts to locate myself within the research were problematic and I do not assume that because I shared 'characteristics' with the women I interviewed – and these sometimes appeared relevant – that this guaranteed insiderness or privileged access to knowledge. Also, although there were aspects of my 'identity' and experience that we shared, there were some which could have been seen as 'other'.

Through the multiple and shifting positionalities of the researcher and participants, it is possible to move across positions and be an insider and outsider simultaneously. It is also possible to be neither an insider nor outsider or for this to be irrelevant. Below l outline my multiple social locations but do not claim that these guaranteed insiderness or precluded outsiderness. Instead, I reflexively address how it was possible for me to be positioned by these women.

I am the daughter of a Somali nomad[9] – the son of a goat and camel farmer – who arrived in the UK as an economic migrant in the 1950s; and of a white working-class woman[10] – the daughter of a farm labourer – from the rural north-west of England. My father has never been formally educated, and my mother did not complete her education, due to family circumstances, leaving school aged 14 without any qualifications. Once in the UK, my father mainly worked in the manufacturing industry in semi-skilled manual roles,[11] while my mother worked in a series of retail outlets since leaving school. In terms of socialisation and cultural acquisition, I consider myself to be first and foremost 'British', having been born in and lived in the UK for all of my life and speak English, but I also feel a Somali identification. As I have argued so far, context is always significant: I have felt and experienced being positioned as 'other'; that is 'not fully British' in the UK, and also as 'not fully Somali' in Somalia. When away from the UK, I have been identified as Greek, Spanish, French, Italian and Indian by others, and also as Russian, due to my first name.[12] In relation to my research participants in Spain, in terms of ethnicity, I could have been simultaneously positioned as both an insider and an outsider. I share the same cultural norms, and demonstrate some degree of national belonging due to the accumulated national capital that I have; but, in terms of bodily inscription (Skeggs, 2004), I could be perceived as an outsider because my skin colour is brown. It is also important to recognise though that 'race' is not the only determining factor, and it may not always be the most significant. Like the majority of my research participants I went to Church of England schools but do not consider myself to be 'religious'. Unlike the majority of the women, I had been in higher education. Being younger, unmarried and childless were also considerations which could mean that I was perceived as 'other': or I may not have been. I recognised that the women shared class, ethnic, gendered and age positionalities with my mother, although they would not necessarily know this.

If the researcher and participants are from the same imagined national community, then awareness of social differences can be enhanced rather than minimised (Ganga and Scott, 2006) and it is important to acknowledge this. Like the women in this study,[13] I was 'from' the UK. However, since I did not live in Spain, I could have been simultaneously both an insider and outsider to the world which the women inhabited. Added to this, I was a 'friend of their friends' which again could have included me (as someone known) and excluded me (as someone strange). Further, although I also shared a gender with the women in my study, and my role in shaping the data generated was significant, it is impossible to say with any certainty exactly what this was since it is impossible to know everything that shapes the construction of knowledge (Doucet and Mauthner, 2008). In this way, my understanding of the women's experiences of migration in retirement is situated and partial, and influenced by my own positionalities and biography (England, 1994).

Conclusion

Women's social locations are apparent in relation to class, gender, age and ethnicity and are differently influenced by context. Translocational positionality is shaped by the meshing of different social locations and in this way each social location becomes altered. Women's gendered, age-related, class and ethnic positionalities are fashioned and reinforced by one another. In this way, 'translocational' refers to the complex relationships between multiple locations: 'the term "translocational" denotes the ways in which social locations are products of particular constellations of social relations, and in terms of relationality and experience at the determinate points in time; it considers them within a spatial and temporal context' (Anthias, 2008, 18).

In this chapter I highlighted the relevant macro contexts which enable retired women's migration to Spain. I unravelled the 'meso context' of women's lives, describing positionalities as a level of interaction between wider structures and women's agency. I developed further my approach to using translocational positionality to capture the relationship between women's gender, age, ethnicity and class and began to place this in appropriate theoretical contexts and within the contexts of their lives. I began to explore the difficulties in disentangling women's positionalities and suggested that understanding the complex relationship between them is key to illuminating their lives in context.

FOUR

Boundary spanning and reconstitution: retirement migration and the search for community

Introduction

> 'Well, purely and simply because someone has had to come up with a word – the word "community" – there has to be such a thing.' (Deidre)

Arguably, all migration is about improving one's life in some way and the women featured here moved to Spain to enjoy a new lifestyle in retirement. For them, a 'better life' involved regaining community and a sense of belonging which had been lost in the UK. Community has been identified as a factor that influences the quality of later life (Conway, 2003) and lamenting the loss of community is a key theme underpinning studies of older people (see Blaikie, 1999; Blokland, 2003; and Savage and Bennett, 2005). In this way, a romantic and utopian discourse around community (Calhoun, 1991) constructs the past as representing a better time and place than the present. Migration involves movement across divides, and for these women, this represents spanning boundaries relating to both space and time in their quest for community. Importantly, boundary markers are key in discourses of belonging and non-belonging (Yuval-Davis et al, 2006), and boundaries are constructed and imposed (Anthias, 2008), shifting and contingent and can be symbolically reconstituted to mark the beginning and end of communities (Cohen, 1985). Boundaries are evident in all types of community, and have been theorised in terms of place, networks and identity. For place communities, there is geographical demarcation, indicating who is from and of somewhere; for networks, exclusion operates in terms of who is 'in' and who is 'out'; and for identity (or positionality) there are real and imagined attributes which signify belonging and non-belonging, operating both in terms of identification and ascription (Ahmed, 2011). I premise that women's quest for belonging and community through retirement migration can be understood as both spanning and reconstituting boundaries in relation to place(s) and networks, shaped by their multiple and overlapping social locations or positionalities across space and time through nostalgia.[1]

In this chapter, my focus is on community, and how focusing on people's experiences of belonging illuminates processes of social change and continuity. I identify retirement migration as a form and consequence of social change which can be understood through multiple and shifting constructions of community. I explain my approach to understanding the relationship between community and belonging and argue that how people construct belonging – and to what – sheds light on how they see themselves in relation to wider contexts. Community is thought to have been lost but is recoverable, and the role of the imagination and the imagery of the idyll are important in constructing it and nostalgia as a cultural resource plays a central role. My focus on different forms of belonging – to place, networks and identity or positionality – is useful in order to understand boundary spanning and reconstitution in the context of retirement migration.

'Thinking with' community to understand social change

> 'We're all in a community here, it's much better; it's much nicer.' (Viv)

Although it is a familiar term, community remains an elusive and contested concept. It is generally accepted that community is a 'good thing',[2] its absence is a 'bad thing', and often, it is 'idealised' (Crow, 2002a). Community represents security, warmth and cosiness (Bauman, 2001); something shared (Cohen, 1985); and solidarity (Crow, 2002a) for its members. Community has been studied across a range of academic disciplines, and can also be understood as 'a fundamentally political concept' (Hoggett, 1997, 14), presented as a policy solution to social malaise (Delanty, 2003; Lemos and Young, 1997) and the integration of minority groups (Mooney and Neal, 2008; Wetherell, Laflech and Berkeley, 2007). The UK context and the use of community in government and policy further exemplify the multi-faceted application of community, drawing on place, interest and identity simultaneously (McGhee, 2005). My aim here is not to critique the success of community as a solution to social problems but to highlight the meta-narrative surrounding community in political and policy circles in the UK in order to frame women's narratives as counter-narratives. I explore this in the second part of the book.

'Community' is constructed, subjective and context specific; encapsulating belonging, similarity or difference, inclusion or exclusion (Clark, 2007). It can be imagined (Anderson, 1983; 2006), social (Amit, 2012), symbolic and utilitarian (Cohen, 1985; O'Reilly, 2000a; Delanty, 2003), concrete and material (Amit and Rapport, 2002) and temporary or 'cocoon'-like (Korpela and Dervin, 2013). Within the analysis presented in this book, community can be ephemeral, tangible and pragmatic, yet its vagueness need not be problematic. Instead, community's ambiguity can be useful to analyse a range of social processes and experiences and be posed as a question rather than a solution: in this way, community is also good to 'think with' (Ahmed and Fortier, 2003).

The search for community is often cited as a motivation to move abroad in migration (Sherlock, 2002; Oliver, 2008), and finding community is often retrospectively put forward as one of the reasons for exercising mobility (O'Reilly, 2000a; Benson, 2012). Community studies have the capacity to pin down in time and space the nature of contemporary social life and place it in context, and also to illuminate the active engagement of individuals and groups in the re-making of their social worlds (Seeley et al, 1956; Crow, 2002a). Examining constructions of community is therefore useful in providing a context for examining representations of social change and for interpretations of human agency (Crow, 2002a; 2002b). Focusing on the motives and agency of individual social actors and the meanings they place upon them (Giddens, 1991) can increase understanding of the 'bigger picture'. Studying community can also illuminate the links between global and local structures, in other words, the study of one's 'own world' within the world (Crow, 2002a; Sherlock, 2002). Often, focusing on the macro level distorts 'lives lived', so looking at the micro level gives us an opportunity to examine how people experience social change (Gillies and Edwards, 2006). For my purposes, using community is useful in order to look at *how* and to *what* retired British women construct belonging in the context of migration. Linking migration to broader theories to enable us to understand social change – in this case community – opens up the processes whereby human agency is shaped by wider structural factors (Castles, 2010). To recapitulate, this allows for an understanding of retirement migration as a form and consequence of social change and allows such processes to be illuminated from particular vantage points.

My changeable use of 'context' requires some clarification. First, it can be used to provide a description of one's own territory or place. I describe women who have moved from the UK to Spain as being 'out of context'; by this I mean that they are away from the country in which they were born. Community in these circumstances can be understood as representing a physical context. Second, I refer to studying community as providing a context to understand macro, meso and micro contexts and social change in particular. Here, I mean community represents a theoretical locus. A further, epistemological consideration is that knowledge is generated within a context, that is, there are cultural, geographical and temporal dimensions that influence and shape such knowledge.[3] Now, I discuss the relationship between community and belonging.

Community and belonging

> 'It's nice to have that sense of belonging, that back up, even
> if you don't need it.' (Celia)

Community can be understood as multi-dimensional forms of belonging (Ahmed, 2011). Although it has been argued that community as a concept is insufficiently nuanced to explain belonging (Huber and O'Reilly, 2004),[4] on the grounds that it neglects people's psychological and social needs, I aim to convince the reader that a multifaceted focus on community has the capacity to explain different forms of belonging in the modern world (Delanty, 2003). It is also useful to look at different forms of belonging to better understand community (Amit, 2012). Floya Anthias defines belonging as being 'accepted as part of a community' (2008, 8), while Vanessa May posits that 'belonging is what helps us connect with the world' (2013, 79). Belonging involves more than affective identification; it is also about acceptance and inclusion (Cohen, 1982). Another way of understanding belonging is to conceive of it as 'a sense of intimacy with the world' (Boym, 2001, 251). Such intimacy with the world, is often represented as community and is considered to have been lost through modernity (Lemos and Young, 1997; Crow et al, 2002; Delanty, 2003).

I put forward my own definition of belonging as *the processes of feeling or being a part of – rather than apart from.* Later in this chapter I discuss this in relation to place, networks and identities or positionalities. The need to unravel the meaning of belonging becomes heightened in the context of population movements and translocation (Anthias, 2006), since we are not usually asked to define what we belong to unless we find ourselves in unusual circumstances (Amit, 2012). Arguably, feeling dislocated in and from the country of one's birth and subsequently being out of context through migrating in retirement represents such 'unusual circumstances' and provides an opportunity to reflect on different forms of 'elective belonging' (Savage and Bennett, 2005) and community. There are also temporal and spatial ingredients to belonging and again context is key. What people feel to be a sense of belonging at a particular time says something about how they see themselves in relation to the immediate – or micro – and wider – macro – contexts in which they are placed in the world (Marsh et al, 2007; Ahmed, 2012).

Community as 'lost'

'I think community has disappeared in England.' (Vera)

This idea of the loss of community can be broadly interpreted in three ways: first, as something that has been irretrievably lost; second, as something that has been lost but can be regained; and third, as something that has yet to be achieved, or as an ideal to strive for. All of these representations of community are 'ideals', since modernity[5] is seen as the enemy of community, with the past as well as community itself being idealised (Delanty, 2003). It is this second representation of community – as something that is lost but recoverable – that is explored and developed through the women's narratives, both in relation to its perceived loss in the UK and subsequent reconstructions in Spain. This second interpretation of the loss of community is a rather more hopeful one – community as *Gemeinschaft*, as a cure for the malaise of modernity for contemporary society or *Gesellschaft*. As Elias (1974) explains:

> The use of the term community has remained to some extent associated with the hope and the wish of reviving once more the closer, warmer, more harmonious type of bonds between people vaguely attributed to past ages. (1974, 23)

Significantly, for the women featured, 'past ages' are imagined and idealised – or 'idyllised' – and evoked with nostalgia. It is useful now to consider in more detail the important role of the imagination in constructing community and belonging, how community is 'idyllised' and how nostalgia evokes community.

Imagined community: a 'sense of belonging'

> 'You're talking about a sense of belonging and a sense of
> community [which] makes you feel safe.' (Margot)

Imagined community has been depicted as a key feature of contemporary society, providing solace against the world, particularly for those in later life, as older people express nostalgia for past communities (Blaikie, 1999) and the women featured construct belonging across time and space through the imagination and nostalgia. The idea of community as imagined is largely attributed to Benedict Anderson (1983; 2006) who conceptualises imagined community in terms of nationality and identity formation, depicting 'the nation' as 'an imagined political community' (2006, 6). For Anderson, 'imagined communities' are located in the minds of 'community members', and there are social consequences to people imagining community in terms of who is in and who is out. However, although the idea of imagined national communities is now well established, it is not without critics, primarily because Anderson's work essentialises belonging, making it one-dimensional, and oversimplifies the complex ways in which people might experience attachment to *multiple* imagined communities (Phillips, 2002). People imagine belonging to other aspects of identity, beyond nationhood (Song and Parker, 1995; Marsh et al, 2007; Ahmed, 2011), and the imagination also constructs belonging to other representations of community which I unravel drawing on the women's narratives.

Conway (2003), drawing on CW Mills (1940), frames imagined community in terms of a 'vocabulary of motive' and motive is represented here as the search for belonging. People's migratory decisions are in part based on their structural contexts and a repertoire of available explanations in popular belief (Conway, 2003). In this way the imagination is also a cultural resource – shaped by context, and in turn it also shapes context (compare Benson, 2012) – not just located in the minds of actors as Anderson (2006) suggests. Motivations to migrate are framed in terms of imagining an alternative lifestyle (O'Reilly, 2007a; Benson, 2012); what is important, as well as imagining the future, the women who participated in my study also imagined a lost past which informed their migratory decisions. The imagination is significant in all representations of community in terms of place, networks and identity or positionality as will become apparent throughout the book.

The role of nostalgia in constructing community

> 'I hoped that the atmosphere that was there during the war would remain. It didn't. Within eighteen months it had gone; yes, just gone. I mean it was there, you were in the shelters it was sort of, and the blitz you know, the blitzkrieg.' (Mabel)

Nostalgia is a relatively modern preoccupation (Boym, 2001), linked to western notions of linear rather than cyclical time, and secular rather than religious societies. Originating from Germany in the seventeenth century, nostalgia was originally a medical term to denote the pain felt by someone who was homesick: *hiemweh*. In the English language it later became known as nostalgia, from the Greek '*nostos*' and '*algia*' which can be understood as nostos, a return home (Boym, 2001; Dickinson and Erben, 2006); and algia, longing (Boym, 2001), or pain and sorrow (Dickinson and Erben, 2006). Svetlana Boym (2001) describes nostalgia as both 'a sentiment of loss and displacement, but… also a romance with one's own fantasy' (2001, xiii) and 'with the past' (2001, 11), while Dickinson and Erben (2006) suggest that it 'is a culturally derived emotion' (2006, 223) rather than a cognitive process, which has both positive and negative feelings. Nostalgia can also be understood to represent the mourning of loss but also an acceptance of loss. In this way, nostalgia has pleasurable and painful connotations and is often linked to notions of innocent childhoods and the countryside, the longing for the home country or a bygone era. Nostalgia has also been described as the 'emotionalisation of absence' (Skrbiš, 2008, 240) in migration.

Nostalgia then can be seen both within the context of and to denote rapid social change, since: 'Nostalgia inevitably reappears as a defence mechanism in a time of accelerated rhythms of life and historical upheavals' (Boym, 2001, xii).

As I have already premised, migration can be understood as a form of social change involving both distance and time thresholds (King, 2012a). When belonging feels fractured or compromised in the present, retired British women look to the past for safety, security and solidarity. Nostalgia therefore represents, for them, a significant part of how community is imagined and constructed. Implicit in nostalgia is that the past represents a 'golden age', since by comparison the present is perceived as 'missing something'. In this way, time and space are linked through nostalgia as are the past and the present. In the previous chapter, I suggested that nostalgia is a chronotope (Bakhtin, 1981), representing the motif of loss, since it links time and space in women's narratives. Now though, I return to community and belonging and their different representations.

Community and different forms of belonging

> 'It's a difficult thing to get a handle on, is community.' (Celia)

In my attempt to pin down different aspects of community it is difficult not to fall into the trap of linguistic essentialism, or iterating 'a belief in the real, true essence of things' (Fuss, 1989, xi). To emphasise, I treat 'community' as having uses rather than definitions as such since I do not think that there are fixed properties. Definitions of community can be seen as interpretations or constructions or partial representations of 'reality' with reference to specific contexts. People experience community in myriad ways and they can belong to multiple communities simultaneously, all of which can be perceived to be in flux (Temple et al, 2005). I unravel my approach to different representations, although it is impossible to completely separate them since place, networks and identities and positionalities overlap. Graham Crow (2002b) argues that:

> Traditional pit villages came closer than any other social arrangement to the ideal type of community in which there is a coincidence of shared place, shared interests and shared identities. (Crow, 2002b, 71)

I aim to persuade the reader that for retired British women living in Spain, that although shared place, interest and identities and positionalities do not wholly coincide, in this context, they are also inextricably linked and reinforce one another. Below, I provide a brief synopsis of these different representations of community, and explore them in relation to women's experiences throughout the second part of the book.

Place

> 'Well community to me I suppose must mean somewhere that you have lived for a long time and you know the shopkeepers' names and you know most of the neighbours' names.' (Joy)

Belonging to place can be understood as an emotional and embodied connection to the world (May, 2013) and community as place suggests living in or feeling belonging to a location in a particular geographical area (MacIver and Page, 1961; Murray, 2000). Often, when community as place is alluded to, it involves studies which take place in a particular geographic location with a focus on specific problems – in this sense data are embedded in the context of community as place (Gillies and Edwards, 2006). Community of place refers to a group of people who are primarily bound together through where they live, although this can also encompass where they work or spend a continuous portion of their time. This has historically been associated with a neighbourhood, village, town or city. For the purposes of my analysis, place refers to both the UK and Spain and to the environment in which women live while in the Costa Blanca, and importantly, the relationships women construct with them and how this influences networks and identity/positionality. Traditionally communities as place have represented a single settlement, although the women in Spain lived in urbanisations in 'several contiguous inner neighbourhoods' (Murray, 2002, 104) rather than a single location.

Networks

> 'To me...a community is a joint effort to get along with each other...community is the mix of people, the joining together of people.' (Cynthia)

Community represented as networks can be understood as being part of the social fabric (Anthias, 2008), relations of social bonding (Sherlock, 2002) or relational belongings (May, 2013) which are often symbolic for migrants in Spain (O'Reilly, 2000a). I suggest that 'network' can be conceived of as both a noun and a verb since it represents the outcome and processes of human agency. Much migration research focuses on the motivations to move and the formation and experiences of social networks and community structures post-migration (Janoschka, 2011; Huete and Mantecon, 2012). In order to understand migration experiences it is useful to focus on social interaction and what is held in common (Amit and Rapport, 2002; Giguere, 2013) along with processes of exclusion and integration (Rodriguez et al, 1998; King et al, 1998; O'Reilly, 2000a).

Women who move to the Costa Blanca in retirement lived in a new, isolated diasporic community, and how they manage to thrive away from established social networks in their country of origin is an important theme. These women manage, negotiate and reconstruct belonging to social networks – including family (Ryan, 2004) – in the UK and Spain, and the role of the imagination is significant regarding networks in terms of imbuing them with certain characteristics over time. Again the role of the past and its influence on the present is important, as we shall see.

Identity or positionality

> 'I see myself as part of a small expat community and that's it.' (Joy)

As I have already discussed, 'identity' is important in discussions of community and migration and there is a symbiotic relationship between identity and positionality and belonging and place and the social (Anthias, 2008). Community need not be a territorial concept nor be contingent on networks or relationships: Milner (1968) refers to the significance of 'community of feeling', which relates to individual and group identification and ascription. Identificational belonging is about boundaries or social locations which shift and change, and some are inscribed in the body (Anthias, 2008), and are also imagined and constructed. In the previous chapter I unravelled the epistemological complexity surrounding identity as a concept and put forward an interpretive approach to understanding the processes involved in identity construction, highlighting that there are numerous 'identities' or positionalities which one could feel and think one 'is', and that these also mediate between wider social structures and agency.

Conclusion

In this chapter I explained that community can be understood to represent an ideal and a solution to social problems and is often imbued with nostalgia. It can also be symbolic, imagined, pragmatic, utilitarian and temporary. It can involve institutional arrangements, relate to policy and has numerous representations, involving different forms of belonging, to places, networks and identities or positionalities. Community is also useful to think with (Ahmed and Fortier, 2003) since it illuminates the contexts in which peoples' lives are lived and processes of social change. Using community to think with in relation to retirement migration allows for an examination of the 'global reconstitution of "community" in different contexts' (Crow, 2002b). Community's concern with boundaries (Cohen, 1985) is particularly relevant since community boundaries are changing and becoming more complex through globalisation and mobility (Mah and Crow, 2011). In the following part of the book I explore retired women's lived experiences of community and belonging through migration to Spain beginning with their motives, agency and decision-making.

Part 2
Lived experiences

FIVE

Leaving the UK: motives, agency and decision-making processes

Introduction

In the previous chapter I suggested that thinking with community and how – and to what – people construct belonging illuminates processes of social change and continuity from particular social locations or positions. Retirement migration was presented as a form and consequence of social change, involving both boundary spanning and reconstitution. The important role of nostalgia as a cultural resource in constructing belonging to different forms of community, evoking an imagined lost place or time, particularly for older people was also considered. In this chapter, I explore the reasons for women's dislocation in and from the UK, and the decision-making processes involved in migrating to Spain. In other words, through the examination of women's narratives, I focus on 'the whys' and 'the how' of retirement migration.

Elements of all three of Halfacree and Boyle's (1993)[1] migrant typologies highlighted in Chapter Two characterise the women featured: they are not easily categorised as singularly purpose rational, traditional or hedonistic. Close examination of women's narratives and how they position themselves sheds lights on motivations, agency in decision-making processes, and how they see themselves and their lives in context and practice. It is now useful to consider how retirement, the high cost of living in the UK, quality of life considerations, and, what is important, feelings of non-belonging due to age and ethnic positionalities shape migration decisions. Women present themselves as rational, traditional and hedonistic in choosing to migrate to Spain in retirement. They cast themselves as fortunate, but not simply through serendipity; instead they are agents who are morally (Goffman, 1959) justified in exercising individualisation through migration (Beck, 1992).

This chapter is structured as follows: first, I examine why women chose Spain as their retirement destination and then consider the multiple reasons for migration in relation to 'a call' (Booker, 2004) which precipitates the quest. I offer a structural analysis of Celia and

Bernice's narrative accounts in terms of how random events occur in everyday adventure time and characterise biographical disruption. I unravel how agency in decision-making in migration is shaped by wider social structures and mediated by women's gendered positionalities, both in relation to those women migrating alone and those with partners. Women's dystopic imaginings of the future and their lived experiences of dislocation in the UK in the present, are considered in relation to the prospect of a poor retirement in the UK and feelings of marginalisation, particularly due to their age and the presence of ethnic 'others'.

Retirement migration: why Spain and not elsewhere

The reasons why people retire to Spain have been well-documented as previously discussed (O'Reilly, 2000a; Oliver, 2008). Retirement as a significant life event (Knox, 1977) embodies new opportunities for the women featured; but it also represents biographical disruption and often triggers feelings of dislocation which can be understood as a consequence of non-belonging (Davidson and Kuah-Pearce, 2008; Ahmed, 2011). Not all of the women identified Spain as their first choice of migration destination, and it is useful to examine the narratives of these women to illuminate why Spain was selected. Decisions to move to Spain rather than elsewhere (Massey et al, 1998) can partly be explained through previous experiences of tourism, coupled with enabling structural forces, for example freedom of movement within the EU (O'Reilly, 2000a), as Myra demonstrates:

> 'It wasn't my first choice. I wanted to go to New Zealand, but trying to get in there is hopeless so I decided to come to Spain.' (Myra)

Myra originally wanted to migrate to New Zealand, but gaining residence is difficult, protracted and time consuming, and probably impossible for someone of Myra's age without family connections there. She presents herself as having agency and as pragmatic, having been thwarted in her attempt to migrate to New Zealand she chooses Spain. Myra would have been happy to move to the other side of the world, but for some women, proximity to the UK and easy access were also identified as reasons why Spain was attractive, as Olive suggests:

> 'I didn't choose Spain. First of all I wanted to go to Greece but it was too far, it was four hours on the plane...this is

ideal, just two hours on the plane and one hour [from the airport]. I can get here in two to three hours from England, so this is why I chose it.' (Olive)

Again, Spain was not Olive's first choice, since she would have preferred Greece, but the journey duration is twice as long as to Spain. Unlike Myra, Olive still wanted to be proximate to the UK. Familiarity was significant for Mabel, and also the fact that the other potential options, Italy and France, were problematic in terms of high cost of living and previous experiences there. For Mabel, nostalgia influenced her choosing Spain; she has happy memories of her childhood there so past experiences are important in shaping her choice of migration destination:

'To Italy? Too expensive. To France? Too many wartime memories. Spain, where I was as a child, as a very small child. I lived with my family in a place called Rio Tinto, there were then copper mines here, our father was one of the engineers who opened it up, electrified it, built a railway and that sort of thing.' (Mabel)

For Phyllis the decision to move to Spain in retirement, rather than their original choice, Cyprus, was influenced by her son and daughter-in-law who moved to Spain to work. This encouraged Phyllis and her husband to rethink their original migration destination. Although her son and his wife decided for them, Phyllis and her husband were very happy with their choice, denoted by 'we haven't looked back':

'Previously we were going to retire to Cyprus but our son and daughter-in-law decided they wanted to come out here to live, and they said "What do you want to go there for? Come out here first," and we did. They decided for us, and we haven't looked back.' (Phyllis)

Phyllis seemed pleased to have her only son and daughter-in-law close by, she and her husband were older migrants, both in their late 70s, so support could have been a consideration for her.

'The call': multiple motivations for migration

Retirement presents new opportunities for the women featured; but it also represents biographical disruption and often triggers feelings of dislocation. Feeling dislocated is also a consequence of non-belonging (Davidson and Kuah-Pearce, 2008; Ahmed, 2011) and this can be understood as being translocated across time and space. There are multiple motivations for migrating (Halfacree and Boyle, 1993), facilitated by upper and more proximate structures (O'Reilly, 2012), but a close examination of women's narratives illuminates their unique experiences, how they position themselves throughout decision-making processes and also how see themselves and their lives in context and practice. All of the women embarked on a quest, although for some the plot shifts to voyage and return which I begin to discuss in the following chapter. Elsewhere (see Ahmed, 2013) I have described the 'call' as 'a note of the most urgent compulsion' (Booker, 2004, 70) in precipitating the quest. In the quest, the central character feels compelled to leave their original home and to set off in search of a new one. It is, however, probably more appropriate to speak of a 'chord' rather than a single note as triggering the quest, since there are numerous reasons prompting women's migration in retirement, as the following excerpt from Deidre's narrative illustrates:

> 'How we came to be in Spain, well, my partner's job was becoming intolerable (1), and then she had a heart attack (2) so we found ourselves faced with a dilemma, what to do next? (3). We thought that it would be a lot cheaper to move to Spain (4), and we fancied a change really (5), a less stressful life (6)…But mainly it was for a better life (7), and a better climate (8) that we moved over to Spain.' (Deirdre)

Deirdre puts forward eight reasons for her and Vera's migration to Spain and casts them as victims of multiple factors, and initially as having little control over their circumstances. Vera's experiences regarding employment, her poor health combined with the opportunity to retire early to a country with a lower cost of living made this possible. Deirdre highlights multiple reasons for their migration to Spain, but the call for them is also about escape to a better life.

Moving to Spain for Olive also involved an element of escape, linked to the circumstances in which she found herself. Olive took early retirement from work, albeit reluctantly, since 'they asked [her] to leave' due to a back injury she sustained at work. However, retirement alone did not precipitate the move to Spain; she wanted to 'get away from the situation', her recent divorce. Olive's narrative illuminates feelings of not being in control of events:

'Myself and how I came to Spain, I'm medically retired; I took early retirement (1) because I injured my back at work and they asked me to leave, so that's the reason (2). I decided to come to Spain just to get away from the situation, for me the situation was that I'm divorced, and to get away from the whole thing I just came to Spain (3).' (Olive)

Olive was disappointed that her employer asked her to leave due to her injury, she would have liked to continue, but was also influenced by the advice from her GP:

'I would've carried on working. I loved every minute of it...I didn't want to finish work. When I asked my GP for advice, he said "If I were you I would take [early retirement], your back's injured, you look after number one."' (Olive)

Very early on in her narrative Enid established that Northern Ireland for her was home and that she and her husband had bought a property in Spain only to escape the poor British weather. She was rather perplexed by people who moved to Spain permanently, suggesting that they were escaping something that had possibly gone wrong 'at home', in the UK. She wanted to make a distinction between herself and these escapees and emphasised that for her, there was only 'one motivation', 'one reason' for buying a house in Spain:

'I think it's maybe, people that are, there's something wrong with home for them. Do you know what I mean? And in what way I don't know, but something at home hasn't been quite right and they've thought, make a new start or something. But obviously permanent residents, well, you see, that doesn't really apply to us. *My one motivation* coming out here was to get away from the British winters. *My one reason*; and I mean if we had the weather at home, I wouldn't be here.' (Enid)

For Deidre, Vera and Olive, something – or several things – *had* gone wrong 'at home', so for them, moving to Spain involved escaping difficult situations which they felt were beyond their control, leading to subsequent feelings of dislocation. Enid quite simply wanted to escape the British weather. For Viv and Myra family was something they wished to escape, although for Viv escaping on a part-time basis was sufficient:

'We've a big family at home and there's always something going on…divorce and what not. It's good to get away sometimes.' (Viv)

Myra presents five reasons for wanting to leave the UK; retirement frames and enables and also provides a trigger to her decision to migrate to Spain, but quality of life, cost of living and the potential health benefits also figure highly.

'I wanted to retire from work (1) and I couldn't retire and live comfortably back in England (2) and my money would go further out here (3)…Plus the warmth (4), I've got arthritis (5).' (Myra)

Ryan (2004) focused on how networks in migration are gendered and how women who migrated from Ireland to Britain managed 'the seemingly competing narratives of compliance and defiance' (2004, 352). She argues that for women, migration and the maintenance of close family bonds – for remittance purposes for example – may reproduce gendered roles. In her study, women did not see themselves as acting alone, but instead needing to fulfil family obligations both in the original home and in the new home by assisting the migration of siblings and supporting family in Ireland. This suggests that family networks often operate in gendered ways, effectively reinforcing gendered roles. Although the women in this study did not send remittance to family in the UK, Ryan's (2004) concept of 'family networks' is a useful analytical tool to understand how migratory processes are gendered. Family could also represent something to escape or a source of support (Ryan, 2004), as is evident through Phyllis', Viv's and Myra's narratives.

Myra wanted to retire early, but could not afford to do so in the UK: she carefully weighs up her options, suggesting a degree of rational decision-making and also agency. In the following excerpt from her narrative Myra presents herself as active, transgressing the gendered role of carer assigned to her and not bending to the will of her family. She talks about her mother becoming 'a bit of a drag' with the implication that she would have been overwhelmed by obligations and duty towards her and that continuing to live in the UK would have made her life 'a real misery'. Instead though, because she escaped, and she has acquired a life in Spain:

'My mother used to ring me up and I had to go shopping in my lunch hour for her, and then it was rush down to her to drop off what she wanted, so like a pressure so it was…She was becoming a bit of a drag. My family thought I should be looking after her…My life was going to be a real misery.' (Myra)

The quests' call: biological disruption and everyday adventure time

The quest's call can be understood in terms of biographical disruption and as such takes place in everyday adventure time (Bakhtin, 1981) which is characterised by random contingency or sudden connecting events. The call represents a disruption since it marks the beginning of a series of events precipitating a move away from what is familiar; the UK, to a new place, Spain. After telling a chronological story about how she and her husband came to be in Spain, Celia begins this part of her narrative with 'then one day', which has a 'once upon a time'[2] quality. The call for her was precipitated by looming retirement and her previous experience of foreign holidays. This excerpt from her narrative is set in everyday adventure time since a series of random temporally contingent events (Bakhtin, 1981) – the retirement lunch at work, the brochure, the exhibition, all 'chance' – combined to encourage a visit to Spain to assess whether she and her husband felt that they could move there. Celia provides narrative linkage (Gubrium and Holstein, 2009) by stepping outside of her narrative to provide contextual information, which is in parentheses in the text, and positions herself as having agency since the final events were not a result of chance since 'we decided':

'Then one day I went to work (I worked for [a large retail store], I'd worked there for 32 years when I retired). I went to work, and one of my friends said (we were at a retirement lunch) and she said, "Oh, we've always fancied going to live near Benidorm." So we sat chatting and I said, "We've always fancied going to live abroad," so she said "Well, actually, we've been to one of these exhibitions for properties and I've got a brochure." I said, "Well, I'd be really interested," and she said "Well, I'm not lending it to everybody 'cos everybody'll want to have a look at it here at [the large retain store] but I know you're interested so I'll lend it to you." And that's how it came about, really. So

she lent me the brochure and she said there's a property
exhibition where I lived in [the UK] and we went to this
one and from there we looked, saw a property, came out.
(We didn't come on an inspection 'cos we said "No, we're
not going on an inspection, they may force us into buying.")
We took a week's holiday and talked to people who had
made this move to Spain. So that's what we did. We booked
a week's holiday and came, and everywhere we went we
stopped, chatted to people, we said, "Do you live here,
what's it like, how do you feel about it?2 And that's really
our start into coming to live in Spain, we decided.' (Celia)

Celia presents her decision to migrate as planned and rational and also
as traditional since the move was based on customs and habits and
previous holiday experiences. For Bernice, like Celia, the call was set
in everyday adventure time. The random events for Bernice and her
husband occurred on a rainy Sunday when the poor weather limited
their leisure options, precipitating a visit to an indoor exhibition of
Spanish properties for sale. The subtext here is that if the weather had
not been so bad then they would have found something else to do on
that particular day. Triggering chance events culminated in Bernice
and her husband exercising agency:

'How I came to be here, it were really rolling really fast
in England and we'd been out to our local for our Sunday
lunch and we said, "What can we do now?" And I said
"There's an exhibition on at a hotel not so far away from
where we live." "Oh well, we'll just go and have a look."
So we went and had a look and the people there were
really nice, there weren't pressure or anything. We got
these brochures and had a good look, a good exhibition it
was. We came home, saw and read everything, looked at
everything and thought, "Umm that'd be alright, shall we
go on one of them inspections and go and have a look?" It
was a horrible day in England and we thought, "We'll go
out and have a look," and then decided to come on a two-
day inspection and bought from there.' (Bernice)

Although there are several random events in Bernice's narrative –
being at a loose end on a rainy Sunday, the nice people, the good
exhibition – she does not present herself as impulsive. Instead, she and
her husband made an informed and planned decision to buy a second

home in Spain. Her memetic use of the exchanges between herself and her husband is a way of stepping outside of her narrative (or diegesis) to provide contextual detail about the process involved in making the decision to buy the house.

The call: agency, gender and decision-making in migration

In considering the role of gender and agency in migration decision-making, I draw upon the household strategies approach as articulated by Hoang (2011), and Chant and Radcliffe (1992). Within this approach, migration decisions are seen as part of household livelihood strategy rather than an individual act; for my purposes here, migration decisions are seen as part of the household's lifestyle strategy characterised by gendered dynamics. It is significant that there are differences in decision-making processes involved for married and single women, and also within these categories, as I now discuss.

Women migrating alone

Olive describes her move to Spain as impulsive, although the previous excerpt from her narrative suggests that she thought through her options in terms of the migration destination. Her use of 'on impulse' in relation to relocating to Spain could be in response to the traumatic life events that were beyond her control: her illness and divorce which made her want to 'get away'. Olive was free to exercise agency:

'I think a lot of people come out to Spain on impulse like I [did]…I didn't plan [it]…it was just last minute. I was ill, divorced, I just wanted to get away and Spain was an option.' (Olive)

For Olive and Margot, as divorced women, there was nobody to contest their decision and no other household members with whom to negotiate; however, as in the case of Myra, there were wider family expectations to negotiate. A further precipitating factor for Margot was the recent death of her father. She presents herself as justified in choosing to leave the UK and as in control of her own life, as she had discharged her daughterly duties towards him:

'So I was selling anyway and I just thought, that's it, I'm off to the warm country…I'd looked after my father…he was 93 when he died last year…so I'd done all that, you know.' (Margot)

Margot presents herself as having agency, being in control, able to exercise individualism, and also as impulsive and hedonistic in her decision, by her use of 'I just thought, that's it, I'm off.' Reflecting back on her earlier comments though, regarding the financial difficulties she was experiencing, moving to Spain was also a pragmatic option to overcome the high cost of living in the UK.

Women migrating with partners

Hoang's (2011) study of gender identity, agency and the influences of intra-household power relations in migratory decision-making in Vietnamese households, is useful in making sense of decision-making processes women who moved to Spain with their partners. Informed by the Household Strategies Approach,[3] Hoang (2011) puts forward four migration categories as follows: consensual, where there is consensus in the household prior to migration; uncontested, where migrants make the decision without gaining consensus from household members, but there is an absence of conflict; negotiated, where any conflict is resolved through negotiation; and conflicted, where unresolved conflict characterises the migration decision. These categories are useful as a starting point, but my analysis of retired British women's experiences develops them further, since they are insufficiently complex to capture the positionalities involved in migration decision making and the dissonance between what people say and how they cast themselves through their narratives.

Agatha, who lives in the Costa Blanca permanently, presents the decision to move to Spain as one made jointly with her husband, with the repeated use of 'we': 'we retired', 'we talked', 'we went to a few exhibitions', 'we thought' and 'we agreed'. Retirement as a framing factor coupled with minor health problems precipitated Agatha and her husband's migration. However, this was not an impulsive move, they had been thinking about what to do in their retirement for several years prior to actually retiring:

'*We* retired officially in England in 2001. *We talked* about our retirement, five or six years before *we* actually retired and what *we'd* like to do. *We went* to a few exhibitions and *we decided* that *we'd* come out and have a look at some properties because *we thought* – *both of us* suffer from various

little rheumatisms and one thing and another – and *we agreed*
on this climate being the best one for *us*.' (Agatha)

Lillian also presents her decision to buy a holiday home in Spain with
her husband as one which she and her husband made jointly, by her
frequent use of 'we':

'Well, *we bought a holiday home 15 years ago* and *we used to
come over with the children*, and after about nine years *we
sold it*, to go and see the world really, going on different
holidays, Australia and the likes of that; and then, four
years ago *we decided we must live round here* and thought we
ought to come back, and bought this for holidays and then
both [husband] and I had to take early retirement last year
through ill health and *we've given it a year to see if we like it
here*, to live.' (Lillian)

From the excerpts from Lillian and Agatha's narratives above, it is
difficult to discern who the main protagonist in migrating to Spain
was; the women or their husbands, or if indeed it was a joint decision.
The decision is presented as consensual, with little need for negotiation
and free from conflict, suggesting that there was a balance of power
within their household, or that they wanted to present themselves in
this way. I revisit this later as women's biographies unfold and they
adjust to their lives in Spain.

Both Cynthia and Joy present their decision to move as being in the
best interests of their husbands. Cynthia acknowledges the multiple
reasons for migrating by her use of 'a variety of reasons', but emphasises
that her husband's health and well-being was the main one, saying this
in five different ways:

'[We moved to Spain for] a variety of reasons, but…my
husband, he couldn't put up with the damp conditions (1),
he's got emphysema (2) and in the damp, the fog, the frosts,
he couldn't do anything (3), whereas here he's got a bit
more quality of life (4) if only because of the temperature,
so consequently he can fare much better (5). So that was
the main reason for me moving over.' (Cynthia)

Similarly, Joy framed her arthritis as being detrimental to her husband,
so deciding to move was presented as being more for his benefit than
hers:

'I have an arthritic problem and I was finding my mobility was becoming stressed which inevitably meant my husband's lifestyle was becoming restricted, so we decided that we would move out to Spain. So, that's what we've done.' (Joy)

Cynthia and Joy position themselves as having agency, but in the context of being 'good' wives: migrating to Spain was ultimately for the benefit of their husbands. From these sections of talk, migration decisions are presented as consensual, again with no evidence of negotiation being necessary and also as free from conflict. Both Cynthia and Joy, through casting themselves as 'good wives' in this part of their narratives raise questions about women's individualism in migration. This is an important point and one which will be developed further.

Agnes' migration to Spain was purely for the benefit of her husband and to improve his health. She edits herself out of the decision-making process and positions her husband as the decision-maker. However, Agnes does not present this as conflictual and she also casts herself as a 'good' wife in this instance through her dutiful compliance:

'My husband was ill, he'd had a stroke, a minor stroke… and the doctor said to him "Oh, you'd be much better off in Spain or somewhere like that."…*He thought it would be a good idea*…At the same time we met friends who were going and *they encouraged him to move*, go and have a look, so we came to have a look and *he was quite happy about it*… so *he thought*, that was what got us going really.' (Agnes)

Similarly, Viv presents her husband's decision to buy a second home in Spain as a joint decision:

'Well, we'd always wanted to come to Spain, not so much me but [husband], when we first came to Spain, you know, when the kids were little.' (Viv)

From the excerpts above, the power dynamics between the women and their husbands are not entirely clear – it could be a taken-for-granted social norm that the husband was the main decision maker and this is therefore presented as consensual. Another layer of decision-making in migration appears to be 'compliance', and this is revisited later when women's narrative positions shift and gendered dynamics are played out in Spain.

Jenny was the only women who presented the decision to migrate as being conflictual. Her daughter and son-in-law originally planned to move to Spain to set up a business and this was key in encouraging her to take early retirement and migrate. Her husband was very keen to live in Spain due to previous experiences of tourism to the area:

> '[My husband] spent a lot of time in Spain with his first wife and always wanted to retire here...Personally I always thought two weeks was enough, but one day, my daughter came to me and asked me... "If [daughter and husband] go over to Spain and start a business, will you come too?" And I said "yes".' (Jenny)

It is highly unlikely that Jenny would have agreed to move to Spain unless her daughter planned to. Celia was also unusual in how she presented the decision to move to Spain with her husband. She appears to have more power in the household decision-making process, rejecting her husband's previous suggestions to move house where they lived in the UK. Although Celia suggests at the beginning of her narrative that she has always speculated about moving abroad, she conveys a sense of surprise that she actually decided to make the move. Here she positions herself as agentic, spontaneous and able to surprise herself as well as her husband:

> 'I've got to be honest; I never thought I'd do it. I've lived in the same house [in the UK] for 28 years. My husband used to say "The only way she'll leave this house is in a box," and I'm surprised he didn't drop dead on the spot when I told him I wanted us to move.' (Celia)

However, it is important to acknowledge that migration is neither purely based on agency or due to macro level forces (Hoang, 2011). For these women, structures enable, and positionalities shape their agency. The motivations and preferences of the women and their husbands in migration may be in conflict or converge and there could also be some overlap between these. The husbands would all have been the main household earner and as such often the 'head of the household' in relation to decision making. In this way, generation/ age, cultural norms, demography, ethnicity and class all shape women's gendered positionalities, their bargaining power and their ability to exercise agency. With the exception of Jenny, and regardless of whether migration decisions were consensual or negotiated, all of the married women minimised or edited out any conflict in the decision-making process or outcome. However, although women generally presented migration decisions as consensual, apart from Agnes who presented herself as compliant – even if their husbands were clearly the protagonist – there are further considerations in relation to negotiating relationships with close family members left behind, particularly with grandchildren. Moving to Spain as a dutiful and loyal wife or in the best interests of the husband challenges the notion that for these women, migration is entirely associated with individualism; however, it can also conflict with being a good grandmother to grandchildren left behind in the UK, as I discuss in Chapter Eight.

Imagining a dystopic future: retirement in the UK

Imagining a 'better' alternative life in a new destination is part of the migratory decision-making process (O'Reilly, 2000a; Benson, 2011a; 2012), as is imagining a 'worse' life in the old one. Further, nostalgia is often part of such imaginings (O'Reilly, 2014). O'Reilly (2000a) usefully identifies the 'Bad Britain' discourse as a resource which people can draw upon to justify and frame their migration decisions, describing it thus:

> Routine; dullness; monotony; greyness; cold; no hope for the future; a miserable old age; misery; modern life; rushing around; no time for pleasure; crime; selfishness; lack of caring; loss of community; lack of trust; poor health; poor education and a poor welfare state. (2000, 99)

The Bad Britain discourse involves a rejection of modern Britain (O'Reilly, 2000a) and importantly for my analysis, 'modern life' is the temporal context in which women experienced dislocation from the UK, in the present. The following excerpt from Myra's narrative captures her feelings and experiences of routine, monotony, rushing around with no time for pleasure and misery in the UK:

> 'In England I didn't have a social life, it was just work, home, cook, wash up and go to bed. Get up the next day.' (Myra)

Cynthia talked about the prospect of an unpleasant retirement, trapped in the UK by using the phrase 'doom and gloom'. These repetitive vowel sounds – or assonance – evoke a sombre and depressing feel.

She used the term 'couch potato' to denote a sedentary, inactive life in front of the television suggesting an un-stimulating retirement and being trapped and miserable. Cynthia's use of the phrase 'looking at the rain pattering' evoked strong visual imagery and she painted a picture of a restricted and poverty-ridden retirement in the UK. This image of misery was described as being compounded by forced inactivity and over-consumption of television while being aware of the elements outside in an almost prison-like state:

> 'If I was in England actually, my vision of retirement in England is just doom and gloom, because all I could see in England was becoming a couch potato, watching TV, looking at the rain pattering down outside the window and sitting in front of the fire. That's all I could think of with retirement and wondering whether I could afford to have the fire on.' (Cynthia)

Mabel also talked about the weather in the UK restricting the opportunities to enjoy a pleasant retirement; rain always seemed to be associated with gloom in the women's accounts. Mabel uses humour, referring to 'a little lace cap and shawl' to characterise an older person from a bygone age and to emphasise even further the prematurely ageing effects of the miserable weather in the UK. Here she attributes Spain with transformation and uses irony: 'all the delights' refers to poor weather and poor health:

> 'I mean, I could've sat at home with a little lace cap and a shawl around my shoulders in the rain and listening to the rain, that endless rain, expecting at this time of the year winter to come, and, with it flu and all the other delights.' (Mabel)

These accounts, by the use of hypothyposis and hyperbole, depict a strong visual image of retirement in the UK as a prison in the rain and in this way the UK was demonised. Margot uses the word 'depressed' twice in a short space of time to emphasise how people are affected by the UK weather. She uses the phrase 'on a treadmill' to describe life in the UK suggesting monotony, routine and arduousness. Margot's reference to people in the UK being less sociable is made with her alliterative use of "grumpy, growly":

'People are very depressed in England. They're on a treadmill of keeping up with everything. They're very grumpy, growly, unsociable, always depressed about something; mostly the weather.' (Margot)

Feeling marginalised: age and ethnic positionalities

Remaining in 'bad' Britain (O'Reilly, 2000a) also represented a threat to some women's values and way of life. Aged 83, Mabel felt very strongly that UK society did not value older people. For someone like Mabel, a highly educated woman who had had a successful career, getting older and being marginalised appeared to be very difficult. Her feelings towards age prejudice come across here in her use of the word 'hate':

'Another thing that I hate in England: age prejudice.' (Mabel)

Mabel's feelings were echoed by Myra and Margot who also felt marginalised due to their age positionality:

'In England there is an age barrier, when you get older, I mean.' (Margot)

'Once you're over 60, you beginning to be on the scrap heap.' (Myra)

Both Mabel and Cynthia seemed angry about being 'forced' to leave the UK. Mabel in particular talked about the political situation and the treatment of older people as factors that encouraged her to move. Her comments about herself as a 'political animal' embody her credentials and intellect and her use of the word 'spin' also shaped how she wishes to be seen. Both are quite 'knowing' terms and Mabel positions herself as media savvy and politically aware and her account shows a level of agency in moving to Spain. Ostensibly, this appears to be about values associated with and linked to a particular place. Mabel put herself in control as someone who had made a discerning choice and has acted upon it:

'Now to come on to the reasons why I decided to emigrate. Well, I'm a political animal and I didn't like the spin and the way things were going in England.' (Mabel)

In the excerpt above, there is a chronological build-up of dramatic tension. Mabel's use of the word 'spin' is also significant: 'spin' often implies disingenuous and deceptive tactics. Politicians are often accused of spin when they claim to be honest and seek the truth while using tactics to manipulate public opinion. However, Mabel did not elaborate further on the 'political atmosphere'.

Cynthia blames immigration and government policy for making life untenable for her in the UK, using the phrase 'gone to the dogs' to demonstrate her disgust at her perceived deterioration of standards: if something has gone to the dogs, it has gone badly wrong and lost all the good things it had:

> 'Personally I think England has gone to the dogs. I think we've allowed too many immigrants which is one of the big problems. Not that I'm racist because I'm not…but I think successive governments are making people racist in as far as giving preferential treatment to ethnic communities and not looking after their own people and I've seen so many things happen in that field and I think it's so unfair and Britain can't afford to do it anymore, there's got to be a limit. I'm not saying that we shouldn't help people when we talk about asylum seekers, etcetera, there are people who I do think we need to help, but the majority that are coming in are not asylum seekers in the true sense of the word and I think successive governments are turning people that way, making people racist just by the fact that they're giving them preferential treatment. They're not contributing anything to the system…if people who were going to move to England and having to provide for themselves, not get everything given off the state and there are very few people now still working to contribute to that, which is proven in the fact that they're now wanting to raise the retirement age, wanting to cut down on healthcare for people who've moved abroad, etcetera etcetera, and it goes on and on.' (Cynthia)

The concept of 'sedimentation' as used by Skey (2011) in relation to discourse is also useful in narrative. Sedimentation refers to 'the process whereby a particular discourse comes to be seen as objective or natural, rather than one possible way of making sense of the world' (2011, 12). Cynthia draws on the cultural dimension of national discourse (Skey, 2011) illustrating how a powerful system shapes and orientates how people see the world as normative. Cynthia begins this segment of her narrative with the use of 'I', then uses deictic language (Skey, 2011), relating to notions of 'us' and 'them'.

Phyllis raises the presence of others – 'refugees' – as making her feel less safe in the UK, suggesting that her life was restricted as a direct result:

> 'We've got, you know refugees…in England…in England we never went out after dark.' (Phyllis)

Phyllis' comment above fits with construction of 'the other': 'where minorities are positioned as a threat to stability, norms and behaviours of a white neighbourhood' (Beider, 2012, 52). This can also be understood in terms of 'stranger danger' (Ahmed, 2007, cited in Lundstrom, 2014) which 'is often posited as originating outside the community, or as coming from outsiders' (2014, 162).

Myra also raises the presence of 'illegal immigrants' as being problematic in terms of welfare services, particularly the NHS. She conveys strong feelings of indignation and outrage about what she perceives as preferential treatment received by immigrants in the UK, saying five times in this short section of talk that she 'resents it':

> 'The illegal immigrants in England, they're coming to take out of the economy…but that's not fair, we do resent it (1). We built up the National Health [Service], I've put into it all of my life and why can't I get something out of it? I mean, I'm lucky, this year I have got new glasses and had my teeth done and I've been to the doctor for my diabetes…but I do resent (2) it because somebody is going to come into the country that has never paid into it, and they're going to live off our money, and I resent it (3), I really resent it (4), I really do (5).' (Myra)

Mabel also highlights her role in 'building up' the NHS in the UK:

> 'It's people like me that built up the National Health Service with 40 years of contributions.' (Mabel)

The issues raised in Cynthia, Mabel and Myra's narratives – negative feelings about immigrants and immigration policy; competition for resources and the welfare state; feelings of unfairness and injustice – resonate with current debates on immigration (most notably by the

UK Independence Party), but it is necessary to briefly explore this within the relevant temporal context, that is when the fieldwork took place (in 2003–04), post-9/11 and the riots in some northern towns in the UK. Influenced by debates on the crisis of a British national identity in academic and policy circles (see Rex, 1996, and Delanty, 1996), an ideology of 'new nationalism' was emerging in the UK. New nationalism was conceptualised, in part, as a media and security construction and a response to the crisis in an overstretched welfare state rather than as cultural superiority (Delanty, 1996). Under New Labour, the position on 'race' and multiculturalism started to shift from celebrating diversity towards the assimilation of ethnic minority groups (Back et al, 2002), and 'community cohesion' policy was on the agenda, representing an instrument of social control and civic obligation for minority groups.

Both Cynthia and Mabel suggest that immigration and the presence of others in the UK are factors that encouraged their move to Spain. Further, the 'influx' of foreigners to the UK was seen to symbolise what was currently wrong there in terms of crime, safety and treatment of the indigenous population. Very soon into her narrative, Cynthia raised immigration to the UK as an issue. She re-emphasises that *she* is not racist, blaming the UK government for people's racism by allowing too many immigrants into the country. Cynthia does not initially draw any parallels with herself and other migrants from the UK in Spain taking over certain areas. It is possible that she was conscious of how she might have been heard by me as a 'brown person', although she presents herself as pragmatic and sensible in her attitude towards immigrants to the UK and not influenced or affected by racist beliefs. I was unsure whether Cynthia was conscious of my 'otherness' at this point since she could have been relating to me as an 'English person', or when she explicitly claimed not to be racist she could be relating to me as someone who might potentially judge her to be a racist. Again, Cynthia's narrative reflects wider popular discourses on immigration (see Dench et al, 2006):

> 'Where I come from it's mainly Pakistanis and they've created their own towns if you like and tried to instil their culture on everybody which is wrong, nobody disagrees. I'm not saying that people shouldn't be allowed to follow their own religion, etcetera, or their own culture, fine, but when you're in somebody else's country, you should follow the rules of that country. Not that I'm racist, because I'm not.' (Cynthia)

When she continues, Cynthia blames immigrants to the UK for her feeling pushed out and apparently speaks on behalf of a majority by her use of 'nobody disagrees'. Cynthia metonymically uses 'we' to represent British people as a whole and presents herself and her argument as reasonable in order not to be seen as 'racist' (Skey, 2011). In the UK, the white working class has been labelled as being hostile to immigration and portrayed as a problematic ethnic group, when the issues could be construed as being about class and how neighbourhoods change – or a sense of place being lost – is experienced (Beider, 2012). However, although anxieties about the presence of others are often attributed to an unreconstructed working class, there is evidence that such sentiments also feature in upwardly mobile groups (Skey, 2011).

Dench et al's (2006) work in Bethnal Green, where the East End is presented as territory which is competed for by different ethnic groups is useful in relation to Mabel. When she talks about immigrants in the UK, she says that 'we' (the state) 'do too much' and 'baby' them with the implication that they receive preferential treatment and as a result 'get the wrong idea' about what can reasonably be expected from their hosts. Her use of the military language, 'retreat and advance' conveys a perceived need to defend territory. Mabel is euphemistic, but suggests that there is a battle or competition between different ethnic groups for territory, or indeed survival. She is aware of how she could be heard and appears not to want to be interpreted as being racist or xenophobic so she edits her talk, positioning herself as a reasonable, measured and fair minded woman, again through the use of humour:

> 'I mean, in England, we perhaps do rather too much and we baby a lot of immigrants and they get the wrong idea. There is a school of thought that can quite easily say, "The more you retreat, the more others advance." I wouldn't like to be xenophobic like the French, but don't quote me on that.' (Mabel)

Conclusion

For these women, dislocation is experienced both temporally and spatially: significantly the quest's call symbolises that 'the times are out of joint' (Booker, 2004; 70), and the original home is 'surrounded by an atmosphere of menace and constriction' (Booker, 2004, 71). In this way, modern life and the UK ceased to represent a time and place of safety or belonging. Women simultaneously cast themselves as victims of wider forces, suffering alienation and psychosocial fragmentation

(Adams, 2007) from the UK in the present[4] and also as agents with multiple translocating positionalities. Women are not easily categorised simply as rational, traditional and hedonistic migrants (Halfacree and Boyle, 1993). Women's migration in retirement can be understood as disengaging from UK society in older age (Rowe and Kahn, 1997), and they choose migration destinations that are congruent with their lifestyle preferences and biographies (Benson and O'Reilly, 2009). Looking closely at women's narratives illuminates how biographical disruption is experienced, how single and married women occupy different locations within gender positionalities, how household lifestyle decisions are made and also how random events can influence outcomes. Women's class position and their age shape their gendered positionality and this is evident in migration decision-making processes. In the following chapter the focus is on women's post-migration lives and the myriad ways they construct belonging – or not – to Spain, the place.

SIX

Living in Spain: 'idyllisation' and realisation

'I don't think there's anything serious that I don't like here.'
(Mabel)

'You're not living a full life here…no, not at all.' (Agnes)

Introduction

In the previous chapter I focused on how my research participants felt dislocated from and in the UK and how their sense of belonging was fractured. Women experienced disengagement from the UK as a place, or space, and also as temporal disjuncture since they also rejected the UK in the present. Age and ethnic positionalities, too, shaped feelings of disruption regarding being on the margins through retirement and the presence of 'others' through immigration to the UK. I unravelled the multiple motivations for women's migration, taking account of structural forces, their unique biographies and agency and positionalities through structurally analysing their narratives, illuminating their lives in context. In order to fully understand women's migration experiences, however, we need to look beyond the circumstances and processes involved in decision making but also at their post-migration lives. Pursuing an individualistic lifestyle is for a privileged few (Skeggs, 2004), and although the women featured are not particularly affluent in the main, it needs to be acknowledged that they were privileged in terms of being citizens of powerful nation states (Benson and O'Reilly, 2009). However, some people have more freedom to make choices than others (Bourdieu, 1984) and women's choices were both enabled and constrained by their previous experiences of mass tourism. Like Benson's (2011a; 2011b) respondents in the Lot in France, women's migration reflects their class position, although this is differently experienced.

In this chapter the focus on place continues. Although global movement is seen by some to have irrevocably changed the meaning and experience of community for older people, it also provides the opportunity to reconsider and examine what it means, particularly in relation to place (Phillipson, 2007). I offer further exploration of how women experience and construct belonging and non-belonging and the complex relationships they have with place, highlighting that it can be imagined, pragmatic and contingent on experiences and intentions. Translocated across space, women construct their Mediterranean idyll[1] imbuing it with nostalgia through pre- and post-migration imaginings of moving to the seaside and eulogise 'good Spain' (O'Reilly, 2000a, 90). Through their narratives, women construct relationships with Spain's physical environment and present multiple reasons for wanting to stay. Living in Spain is presented as transformative, Spain itself as 'exotic', yet like the UK, but in the past: in this way, they are also translocated across time. Looking at different experiences in terms of how women manage – or not – to overcome certain obstacles[2] once in Spain, and how some manage heterolocal lives, provides unique insight into how they differently experience migration in retirement. In this chapter, obstacles identified through thematic analysis of women's narratives are discussed here in relation to managing 'temptations' and living on an urbanisation.

Community idealised

"I think community is idealised and romanticised because we all need a feeling of safety and security." (Vera)

As I have elucidated, community is often represented as something of a utopian ideal and there is a romantic and nostalgic discourse surrounding it, centring on its loss and recovery (Delanty, 2003). The past often represents a better place (Blaikie, 1999) or a lost paradise (Bauman, 2001) and can also be used as a resource (Cohen, 1985), in this case, to escape the present. Evoking community can be understood as resisting modernity and often, too, migration is conceptualised as counter-urbanisation or anti-modernity (O'Reilly, 2003; Halfacree, 2012) through the construction of an 'idyll' almost suspended in time (Waldren, 1996). Counter-urbanisation and the search for an idyll (O'Reilly, 2000a; 2003; 2007a) can also be understood in terms of nostalgia, since they reflect a rejection of the present and seeking solace in the past.

Notions of an 'idyll' are usually represented as moving to the countryside or seaside. My interpretation of an 'idyll' is that it represents an idealised place to strive for or recreate; somewhere tranquil and unspoilt by modernity (Pahl, 1966; Newby, 1980; Rye, 2006) and this relates to networks and identity as well as place, since 'a dense social structure' (Rye, 2006, 2) characterises the idyll. The idea of moving to the seaside is imbued with myths and propaganda rather than an historical reality – particularly among older people who appear influenced by a range of symbolic meanings which ritualise community (Blaikie,1999). An idyll can therefore be understood as representing another place and the same place in another time, usually the past. The desire to live in a beautiful landscape reflects the desires of lifestyle migrants (Waldren, 1996; King et al, 2000; O'Reilly, 2000a; Benson, 2012): it is worth noting however, that such positive characteristics are bestowed upon places, rather than being intrinsic to them.

Idyllising Spain

> 'In Spain there is lovely food, fruit, vegetables, people, sociable, sunny, smiling; just a happier environment.' (Margot)

The UK no longer represented somewhere that belonging and community could be achieved and in part, this led these women to set out on a quest for an alternative: Spain, which was presented as a place where community and belonging were possible. The construction of Spain as an idyll (Blaikie, 1999; O'Reilly, 2000a) involves 'an idealised attachment to the local natural environment' (Sherlock, 2002, 8); time slows down and there is a melding of human life and the natural environment (Bakhtin, 1981). Mabel, for example, uses dramatic language to demonstrate her feelings about Spain. The use of 'savage beauty' and 'excitement' also evokes a sense of joy in the unknown in relation to Spain. Through her use of hypothyposis, Mabel presents herself as almost childlike in her enthusiasm, demonstrated by her use of the word 'love' three times in relation to the 'flora and the fauna'; 'the excitement' and 'Spain' itself:

> 'It has a kind of savage beauty that I like. I love the flora and fauna. I love the excitement of finding a praying mantis in my garden. I love Spain.' (Mabel)

Mabel is enchanted by Spain's natural environment and also romanticises and eulogises its past:

> 'I love its history. I'm a kind of spoiled Roman Catholic. This is the land of Toquameda, the Inquisition, it's a land

of violence and romance, civil war and beautiful places to see.' (Mabel)

Olive talks about the restorative and contemplative properties of the sea, showing a communion with the natural environment. She casts herself as being in tune with the rhythms of nature (Halfacree, 2014), and her moods and emotions are soothed and enhanced by being by the shore:

> 'The sea…if I am feeling down…or when I'm happy I always go to the waterside.' (Olive)

Other women also constructed Spain's natural environment as having positive impacts on well-being, mood and behaviour. A distinctive feature of the idyll is that there is a 'conjoining of human life with the life of nature' (Bakhtin, 1981, 226) and the use of metaphorical language to evoke it. For example, Joy lauds the 'sunshine and blue sky' evoking strong visual imagery and the weather is presented as an analogy of behaviour. People are 'more cheerful' as a result of feeling better. This is contrasted with people being 'screwed up with cold and misery' in the UK; the cold weather is seen as responsible for making people physically ill and detrimental to mental health. The use of the phrase 'screwed up' has a double meaning suggesting an individual's defensive physical stance against the cold but also denotes mental distress, illness or dysfunction. Joy talks as though her feelings are universal, common sense and natural by her use of 'of course':

> 'You just automatically of course feel better from seeing the sunshine and the blue sky and everybody's more cheerful. That's really the most positive thing about being here. You feel better because you're not screwed up with cold and misery.' (Joy)

Myra too talks about the Spanish climate and its impact on people's mood, well-being and behaviour, saying that the UK weather made people 'repressed'. On first reading I thought this was a malapropism and she actually meant 'depressed' but the parallel is that in Spain people are much more outgoing, cheerful and more willing to engage with one another than they are in the UK. Here she idyllises Spain:

> '[In Spain] … everybody is much happier. Everybody you meet is more outgoing than they are in England. I think the

weather makes them repressed where here; no, everybody smiles at you, everybody talks to you.' (Myra)

The physical aspects of Spain are talked of in relation to their positive influence on people's behaviour. Women talk generally – that is, in terms of other people – and also in relation to themselves. The weather and Spanish environment are perceived to have favourable impacts on people's emotions and conduct, so in this way place facilitates well-being, mood and interaction. For these women in the Costa Blanca, then: 'Idyllic life and its events are inseparable from this concrete, spatial corner of the world' (Bakhtin, 1981, 225). The connotation is that living in Spain is potentially transformative: migration represents a transformational experience (Williams, 2005). This is particularly apparent for Mabel:

'Look at me here! I'm ten years younger!' (Mabel)

For Mabel, being in Spain is rejuvenating, making her feel 'ten years younger'; and I was cast as someone who could bear witness to her claim by the use of 'look at me here'. Selecting a new physical location can reaffirm identities and goes some way to explaining why people choose alternative destinations in old(er) age. Belonging and identity are linked to community and place (Phillipson, 2007) and place and physical environment have an influence on constructions of the ageing self (Wahl and Lang, 2004).

The idyll as freedom

Spain also represents a context which provides the opportunity to exercise freedom. For Myra with respect to having more time for herself and being free from the demands of others; and for Mabel, in terms of not being encumbered by the UK's political environment.

For Myra, time slows down in the Mediterranean idyll (Bakhtin, 1981). She can enjoy doing what she chooses to do:

'Now I've got all day to do what I want to do, and normally go out in the evenings, or we go on trips; we go on trips to some of the local beauty spots. It's a much slower way of life, but I'm doing a lot more really.' (Myra)

This resonates with Oliver's (2008) study, where time is experienced as something that is less hurried yet needs to be filled in order to age positively.

In Mabel's earlier comments about being a 'political animal', she demonstrated both agency and sentience and that she was engaged but disillusioned with the UK as a place. For her, Spain embodies an escape from such restrictions. Women's talk contains key images of the UK as restrictive and Spain was eulogised as offering freedom. In the excerpt below, Mabel presents living in Spain as being free from caring about politics:

> 'I came to Spain for something else too, my ignorance of Spanish politics … It's not my country, but that's just a bonus because I can't give a monkey's what's happening politically. I have freedom.' (Mabel)

For Mabel, being ignorant of Spanish politics, not belonging to Spain – and Spain not belonging to her – allows her the freedom not to care yet this does not detract from her love of Spain.

The idyll as an adventure

For some women, living out of their country of origin was exciting and an unexpected undertaking. Even though Vera did not plan to stay in Spain, she used the words 'exciting', 'challenging' and 'thrilling' to describe living there. Here, the unknown and unfamiliarity of living in a foreign country are significant and there is a sense of adventure:

> 'I do like the fact that within 20 minutes I can be down by the Mediterranean. There is, there is something about living in a country that has a different language, there's something quite *exciting* about it. There's something quite *challenging* about trying to understand what people are saying to you in a different language. There's something about being resident here that's quite *thrilling* you know.' (Vera)

Vera presents multiple reasons for experiencing Spain as an adventure. She conveys a sense of being out of context, away from the UK, as exotic, in relation to a different physical environment, language and people. At this point in her narrative, Vera focuses on the positive aspects of living in Spain: indeed, in the voyage and return plot, in the early stages 'at first the strangeness of this new world…may seem diverting, even exhilarating, if also highly perplexing' (Booker, 2004, 87).

Regaining community and a sense of belonging in Spain

'It's like England used to be here in Spain.' (Myra)

A significant way that women idyllised Spain was to present it as being like the UK was in the past. This was done in a number of ways. Vera talks about a 'sense of community' present in the UK of the past:

'In England when I was growing up there was a bit of a sense of community...when people were all in the same boat and things were quite bad and people had sort of pulled together through the war...but over the years I think that sense of community has died.' (Vera)

This sense of community is a feeling; it is intangible, elusive and a response to common hardship precipitated by shared experiences of the Second World War.

Community here represents 'belonging' and people 'pulling together', and a sense of belonging can engender a feeling of safety, and, although both belonging and safety are ephemeral – or imagined – they are also simultaneously experienced as 'real' and used pragmatically when necessary. Vera's narrative illustrates that place is still the context where belonging is experienced. She idealises the UK in the past and draws parallels with Spain in the present, thus linking time and space chronotopically through nostalgia:

'Coming to Spain, I actually feel that that community to some extent has come back but again it's through, if you want to use the word, adversity, in the sense that you're living somewhere where you don't know where to go for help...you don't know the language, this that and the other. You rely on each other, so from that point of view I do feel a sense of community here.' (Vera)

She uses the first person singular and then plural to signify the perceived inclusiveness that 'community' engenders. Vera talks of 'everyone being in the same boat' in Spain – denoting a shared experience or exclusion through not speaking the host's language – creating a sense of isolation from wider Spanish society. For Vera, moving across space through 'coming to Spain' is interchangeable with moving across time since community 'has come back'. There is an orientation to the past to evoke and construct a sense of safety, belonging and community, and: 'with this nostalgic glance Britons impute to Spain traits which they consider were part of historical Britain' (O'Reilly, 2002, 182–3; see also Benson, 2012).

A sense of community in the UK during the period following the Second World War is compared to contemporary Spain in terms of there being something to mobilise against. Both periods are synonymous with hardship, although the nature of such hardship differs. Vera conveys a sense of ostracism, by being out of context; evoking community is therefore a reaction to hostility and threats and constructing and perpetuating a belief in it emerges as a defensive strategy. Community is also seen to be arrived at through adversity in that migrants have to work hard to thrive in their new environment. Mabel, too, draws comparisons between the community-minded atmosphere during and following the Second World War in the UK and life in contemporary Spain:

> 'It reminds me of the London blitzkrieg in the Second World War...Why did that die? Everybody was friendly, everybody thought that tomorrow they might be dead – not that we think that in Spain – but it was a kind of camaraderie, which is quite prominent here in Spain...I found it again in Spain.' (Mabel)

In Mabel's talk there is again a time and space dimension; during the war in the UK the atmosphere 'was there' and then it 'was gone'. However, decades later, she found it again, in Spain. Both Vera and Mabel are rather wistful about the loss of community in the UK. They discuss it in terms of 'community spirit' and 'atmosphere' almost as if it is ephemeral, although it does seem 'real' in that its presence was 'felt' – it was 'there', then it had 'gone'. Both women feel that community for them has been recovered in Spain, for Vera it has 'come back' and is 'here', and Mabel again talks about the atmosphere which evoked that which was present during the Second World War. Although they use opposing adjectives – 'adversity' and 'camaraderie' – they are talking about the same thing but from different perspectives. Vera feels that a sense of community in Spain is brought about as a cohering force stemming from (perceived) adversity since migrants are not part of mainstream society; while Mabel focuses on the effects of such cohesion depicted as 'a kind of camaraderie' in the excerpt above. In Vera and

Mabel's account there is an orientation to the past through nostalgia and recollections of the past shape understandings of the present. This contrasts with Oliver's (2008) study of retirees to the Costa del Sol, where people manage the tensions between positive ageing and the body through an orientation to the present. Nostalgia is most apparent in the women's accounts when they talk about the sense of 'community' experienced in Spain being reminiscent of past times in the UK. Women represent community as something that has been lost through modern life in the UK but recovered – by them – in Spain. Lamenting the loss of community in the UK can be understood as an indictment of the UK in the present and a valorisation of Spain in the present: as a haven suspended in time.

Obstacles to living 'the good life' in Spain

Initially, all the women were positive about moving to Spain, the negative associations of the idyll were absent and instead the focus was on ease, wellbeing and enjoyment: in other words, a place where the good life could be practised. However, in order for the quest to be fulfilled, certain obstacles need to be overcome. Booker (2004) presents four categories of obstacle standing between the central character and the quest's goal: 'monsters'; 'temptations'; 'deadly opposites" and 'the journey to the underworld'. All of these represent ordeals of some kind: the significant one for the women featured are 'temptations', which appear here as succumbing to the trappings of a holiday-like lifestyle or being enervated by the heat.

Temptations

'We're all lotus eaters here.' (Joy)

Joy's comment above, describing British migrants to Spain, refers to the Greek myth, the Odyssey, and the land of the lotus eaters. The original lotus eaters existed in a semi-comatose stupor, unable to do anything because they had eaten narcotic lotus leaves. Mabel acknowledges the potentially debilitating physical effects of being in Spain, but through being able to recognise the 'trap', she is able to overcome the temptation to 'lie back':

'Spain has a habit of making you lie back and think "Aah."
That's the trap.' (Mabel)

While Agatha, although acceding that there is a relaxed holiday atmosphere in Spain, is keen to emphasise that this is not how she and her husband choose to live and that she also avoids the trap of succumbing to its potentially tranquilising effects:

> 'It's like being on holiday all the time here. I mean we don't treat it like that.' (Agatha)

Nevertheless, some of the women who move to Spain do so in part for a hedonistic lifestyle, as Margot suggests

> '[There's] so much to see in Spain; the beautiful bars where you can get inebriated very quickly…it's just a different type of life.' (Margot)

There was recognition among some women, however, that this kind of lifestyle was not sustainable and that it could be counter to a healthy and happy retirement as Celia explains in the excerpt below. Celia refers to 'this quality of life'; implicit here is that it is better than the UK. She refers to health twice, suggesting that Spain is a healthier place (physically and mentally) to live. Celia's comments below echo a number of conversations I had with people living in the Costa Blanca. Almost every person I spoke to mentioned that the World Health Organisation had designated the Costa Blanca as one of the healthiest places to live in the world. When this was recounted, it was often done in such a way that suggested that by merely living here people would benefit, almost by osmosis. There did not seem to be any recognition that lifestyle, diet and excessive consumption of alcohol rather than just physically being in a place were significant, although Celia acknowledges this:

> 'We've got this quality of life, always sunny, we want to keep healthier, because it's supposed to be really good. The World Health Organisation say it's one of the healthiest places, provided we don't get to be alcoholics.' (Celia)

Deirdre and Celia also recognise the potentially enervating effects of being in Spain, this time in terms of the weather. However, the narrative strategies that women employ when they talk about managing the effects of the hot weather and how they position themselves reflect their experiences and future intentions: whether or not they wish to remain in Spain. For Deirdre, the heat is incapacitating, difficult to tolerate and prevents her from doing anything:

'The heat…it's just been awful…you can't do anything.' (Deidre)

Yet Celia minimises the impact of feeling bored through forced inactivity due to the heat, by emphasising the temporary nature of such restriction. After all, Celia plans to stay:

'I've been bored with the heat…but now we're coming out of it, we're into September, it's cooling off a little bit. I think the evenings have been a little bit cooler.' (Celia)

The ways that women cast themselves through their narratives in relation to overcoming (or not) 'temptations' resonates with whether they plan to remain in Spain or return to the UK. The linguistic devices used regarding how women experience and adjust to living on an urbanisation also reflect and construct experiences and future plans. Time slowing down and the *mañana* stereotype (O'Reilly, 2000a; Oliver, 2008) are also related to a sense of timelessness or idyllic time as Mabel's narrative suggests:

'This is the country of *mañana, mañana*. But tomorrow never comes and neither do the workmen!' (Mabel)

Living on an urbanisation

'I would say, when I was coming out [to Spain] that I didn't realise what it would be like living on an urbanisation.' (Celia)

Although women idyllised Spain on spatial and temporal levels: as a place, in terms of its natural environment; and also with respect to 'time', since it was constructed positively as how the UK used to be (see also O'Reilly, 2003), the reality of living on an urbanisation was an obstacle with which most of the women struggled. In this way there was incongruity between women's pre-migration imaginings about place and their lived experiences (see also Benson, 2011b, and Halfacree, 2014). It is useful here to consider two opposing depictions of Spain – the place – highlighted by Caroline Oliver (2008) in her study of British retirement to the Costa del Sol. The first is from an autobiography written by Hugh Seymour-Davies (1996) and portrays Spain as idyllic and peaceful; while the second, from JG Ballard's fictional *Cocaine nights* (1997) presents the environments where British people live as soulless artificial leisure worlds, disembodied from 'real Spain'. Oliver describes both of these representations as 'colliding' in her ethnographic account of middle-class British retirement migration to a Spanish *pueblo blanco* (white village). For my research participants, their experience of the idyllic depiction was largely limited to the imaginary realm, since their reality was living among other 'residential tourists' on mass purpose built urbanisations on the margins of Spanish society. The Costa Blanca saw unprecedented development from the late 1990s, with much of the coastal region built on. These developments are not linked to the established Spanish towns rather they are on the peripheries of established infrastructures, and the modernisation linking tourism and the property market in the Costa Blanca is characterised by a distinct lack of planning (Huete et al., 2008). At the time of the fieldwork, there was little regulation from the Spanish Government about building density and both Joy and Lillian were critical of such unregulated development:

> 'There is just too much building going on in this costa. The Spanish government seem not to have learned the lesson of leaving the sea open to be seen. So you could be living anywhere in the middle of all these buildings.' (Joy)

> 'Well we bought this [house] off plan, and we'd driven past, used these beaches 15 years ago…all this area was just shrub land, or agricultural, or orange groves, lemon groves…and then we came back, we were conned along with a lot of other people. We came back I think it was 18 months later and we could not believe the development…I think the Spanish government should have taken control and made some guidelines. They've just let the builders do whatever they want…and that I think is very wrong.' (Lillian)

In Spain, typically, a builder acquires land privately and then builds houses and roads on it and an agent then goes on to promote and sell the properties on behalf of the builders. Several women talked about the agents acting unethically as the excerpts from Mabel and Vera's narratives suggest:

'One thing I didn't mention, the people who sell the houses. Now some are fabulous, a lot are fabulous, but some want to sell houses and I am afraid they are creating problems for people that should not have these problems. There's no telephones, sometimes no roads, sometimes no contact, sometimes no ability if they don't drive to get to a supermarket.' (Mabel)

'People get pushed into certain areas through the agents.' (Vera)

Agents like housebuilders therefore, can be understood as a 'more proximate structural layer' in lifestyle migration (O'Reilly, 2012), and operate both in terms of enabling – making affordable houses available; and also constraint, due to location, design and remoteness of the urbanisation, effectively creating physical and symbolic boundaries. Living on urbanisations also shapes the type of networks that women form and how their ethnic positionalities are reconstituted, as I discuss in the following two chapters. For Agnes, the remote location of the urbanisation was problematic, particularly when compared to where she lived in the UK:

'I can't just pop down the town when I want to; living on an urbanisation I don't like.' (Agnes)

'[In the UK] we lived near to *the doctor*, near to *the chemist*, near to our little *cottage hospital*, near to *entertainment*, we had *theatre* and we had *cinema* and we had a good *library*, near to *the station*, near to *the buses*.' (Agnes)

Unlike the detached dwellings on the Costa del Sol and the Costa Blanca described by Huber and O'Reilly (2004), most of these women lived in 'quad houses' which were effectively four back-to-back 'villas' contained in one building, each with a roof terrace and small front garden, with an open area at the front of the property. Most people turned this area into a small dining space since the interiors were not large enough to accommodate a dining table and chairs. Typically, these houses had a bedroom and bathroom on each of the two floors and an open plan lounge and kitchen area on the ground floor. All of the women in this study lived across four purpose built urbanisations, within approximately one square mile. Within this area, there were four shopping malls with restaurants, bars, pubs and small convenience stores. There were two large supermarkets within a three mile radius. There were several Chinese, Indian and Italian restaurants, but no Spanish restaurants. The bars and pubs were English or Irish and the convenience stores stocked British goods.[3] This was unproblematic for some women, like Myra:

> 'One Chinese we go to it's four euros 95, which means a starter and a main course, plus half a bottle of wine, plus free drinks when we go in, plus free prawn crackers, plus free schnapps at the end. For four euros 95! Try and do that in England.' (Myra)

Others, however, expected a more 'authentic' Spanish experience. Enid and Vera expressed disappointment at not living a more Spanish life. The educational background of the women is also significant; those who were better educated and with more cultural and social capital wanted a more 'authentic' experience. Enid's disappointment centred on the reality not living up to her expectations of Spain – she hoped that she would gradually be integrating into Spanish society. When she mentioned 'a caricature of Magaluf', a stereotypical British holiday place in Majorca, which she saw as a parody of British life, she makes it clear that that was not what she was looking for. Her use of 'you need' suggested it was in fact what the majority of migrants from the UK actually wanted:

> 'I expected to live a more Spanish life you know…you have to go four miles into Torrevieja to go to a Spanish restaurant.' (Vera)

> 'I did sort of think to myself, you know, we'd be living in a wee Spanish village going to little Spanish restaurants. It's like, it's like a caricature of Magaluf where you know, you need your fish and chip shop and you need your sports pub.' (Enid)

The quest for authenticity, most often associated with middle-class identification practices (see Benson, 2011a) was not something most women in this study talked about; instead they focused on being able to exercise freedom and to enjoy 'Spain'. Authenticity captures the built and natural environment and also the psychosocial dimension: culture, value, beliefs and behaviours, and arguably has never been a feature of mass tourism. Authenticity relates to those elements that are original, simulated or imitated. During the 1970s, debate centred on whether it was possible to have authentic experiences in tourism (Mantecon and Huete, 2007), although authenticity is not usually a central feature: Instead, experiences, different from the mundane are considered important (Urry, 1990). Although some women identified with 'Spain', the place, they could not claim to live authentic Spanish lives.[4] Authenticity was not a design feature in their neighbourhoods in the Alicante province (Huete and Mantecon, 2012). Instead there was a 'staged authenticity' (MacCannell, 1973; King et al, 1998) which enabled the women to live the kind of life they wanted in a place which allowed them to, so in many ways, it was more about this than the place itself (King et al, 1998).

Sharing space with holidaymakers

It is well documented that British migrants do not identify as tourists and wish to disassociate themselves from them (see O'Reilly, 2000a; 2003; Oliver, 2008; Benson, 2011a). For the women featured in this book, it was not just about identification, but also relates to territory since they lived in such close proximity to tourists who rented properties on their urbanisations. The design of the houses was also considered problematic as there were issues with noise:

'A lot of these are holiday rentals and you get the inevitable Falaraki[5] situation of drunks and things during the season.' (Joy)

'There's just one thing I've got against it and that is some of the lets. They mess things up and the walls are so thin you can hear everything.' (Phyllis)

Being on the committee of the urbanisation

'I'm on that darn committee but I'm coming off it 'cos I can't stand the people that are on it.' (Enid)

Each urbanisation is split into a number of 'irias' (areas). People who buy a house from an agent individually own their property, but each urbanisation collectively owns the road and amenities. Maintenance of these is paid for by fees levied from all of those residing there. Each iria should have a president, a vice president and often (but not always) a committee. The president and vice president – who in theory should be elected with the help of the committee – manages the urbanisation in terms of road and amenity maintenance. Each iria employs and pays a Spanish administrator (again paid by the annual fees levied) and the administrator is chosen by the committee. The role of the administrator is to provide legal and financial advice and basically to act as a conduit between Spanish agencies and the committee. Committees usually meet monthly and there is an annual AGM open to all residents.

Vera and Enid sat on the committee for their urbanisation and felt very strongly that it was a corrupt and unfair process, attracting the wrong kind of people. They were the only women on a committee of 14. Both felt that their experience on the committee was negative and that they were marginalised by the majority male cohort. This was made worse by the fact that the committee appeared to be ineffective in making decisions or representing the interests of the people living there as Vera's comments suggest:

> 'I'm on the committee of the urbanisation which is one of the most undemocratic things I've ever come across.' (Vera)

Vera told the story of an argument between the committee and the president of an urbanisation. The committee itself was comprised of English and German members while the president was German: the president being German was seen by many committee members as problematic since there were very few German people living on the urbanisation. The argument centred on heating the outdoor pool and the necessity of installing hot showers. There was disagreement from some of the British members of the committee regarding the need for and cost of these showers, while the president was insistent on their installation. The ensuing argument moved away from the issue of the showers to something altogether more serious, as Vera explains:

> 'The German president said that we will build showers, so of course somebody then said, "Yes, well, we knew what happened when you bloody lot built showers last time." And the whole thing sort of then fractured down the middle between the Germans and the English.' (Vera)

In the excerpt above, Vera's use of the word 'fractured' suggests that the illusion of community was shattered and that national divisions became apparent as a result of deep-rooted tensions. Vera suggests that it was something rather fragile, so, although she believes community is important and 'exists' in Spain, there was precariousness to it. Her use of 'so of course somebody then said' conveyed sympathy with the circumstances and perspective of the 'English' members of the committee; after all, Vera was herself English and she presented herself as loyal and patriotic through her talk. Here, the past influences the present and Vera talks from the general to the particular. This example proves her point:

> 'There are there are these kind of underlying tensions that can come out…Even though I've said that there is a sense of community here, there are odd times I think it could factionalise, things can get quite fractured, particularly between Germans and English. Old bitternesses die hard.' (Vera)

Conclusion

Place can be idealised and imagined on several different levels; first there was an idealised attachment to Spain's natural environment (Sherlock, 2002) linking to a romantic and utopian attachment to the Mediterranean idyll; and Spain, the place, also represented a better quality of life which entailed escape and freedom from responsibility. The women featured related to Spain in a selective way; it represents escape and community but they do not engage with the reality of modern Spain (King et al, 2000). Further, women's place-making practices are material and semiotic and there is a dialectical relationship between people and place (Torkington, 2012). Additionally, 'places are fluid and shifting rather than static entities and, like people, they can have multiple identities' (Torkington, 2012, 75).

People construct belonging to places to provide a physical context for their lives. What women chose to focus on and how they present this highlights their perceived differences between the UK and Spain. Spain, in the present was certainly idealised and imagined by all women before they moved to Spain, rather like they imagined an England of the past. Once there, some women changed their view of Spain, since the gap between the real and the imagined was too great and this is where plot shift begins to emerge. Those women who wished to return to the UK were unable to overcome a number of difficulties, including being out of one's familiar context, or place. A narrative approach is useful in analysing *how* women construct belonging and how they position themselves in relation to places. In the following chapter the focus shifts to how the women construct belonging to networks and how their social interactions are shaped by their social locations or positionalities.

SEVEN

Belonging to networks: reconciling agency and positionalities

> Many British seek their own wherever they go, but perhaps with more enthusiasm than other nationalities. (King et al, 2000, 148)

> 'There's a lot of English, isn't there, around, and I think they seem to, they always seem to be with the English, don't they?' (Jenny)

> 'All our friends here come from England.' (Agatha)

Introduction

In the previous chapter I focused on how the women featured experience and narratively construct belonging and non-belonging to Spain and the complex relationships they have with place(s), highlighting that such associations can be imagined and pragmatic, shaped by social 'locations', and also contingent on experiences and intentions, or the end point of plot movement (Bakhtin, 1981). In this chapter, the core theme is networks and their connection with spatial, temporal and social locations. I explore how geographical location – where one is from and where one is located – is significant in shaping belonging to networks and how women's networks in the Costa Blanca are also influenced by and reflect their class, age, ethnic and gender positionalities. These retired British women, living in tourist spaces reinforce some of the negative media representations that O'Reilly (2000a) and Oliver (2008) dispel, since they do not integrate with their hosts or attempt to speak Spanish and their consumption habits are typically British and orientated to the past. In Chapter Three I described migration as spanning boundaries and argued that women also reconstituted boundaries once they arrived in Spain. Boundaries are particularly apparent in relation to the kinds of networks in which women engage and how they construct these through their narratives.

This chapter begins with a description of women's 'social scene' in the Costa Blanca and presents a discussion of how women with partners and lone women engage in social contact. This is followed by an examination of how married women differently experience and manage the increased amount of time spent with their husbands in retirement. I then present the Silver Ladies club as an example of a gendered social network and lifestyle-based gathering, translocating with class, ethnicity and age. The role of language as constructing and reflecting women's experiences is then considered in relation to social locations and constructions and reflections of Englishness as an ethnic positionality. I go on to explore how living an English life in Spain is for some women a further obstacle which cannot be overcome and conclude by examining how women 'other' the Spanish and how this reinforces and reproduces their own positionalities.

The 'social scene' in the Costa Blanca

As I have suggested elsewhere (see Ahmed, 2011; 2012), in diasporic circumstances, it is practical for retired migrants to form networks. Women are away from family and friends in the UK and need quest companions to assist in achieving the life renewing goal of belonging and community, and they cannot achieve this with their hosts. Although these women have been living in the Costa Blanca for a relatively short period of time, since this was a new social setting for all them, it is possible to become quickly embedded in networks formed though lifestyle-based gatherings (O'Reilly, 2000a; Sherlock, 2002; Ahmed, 2012). This runs counter to findings from traditional community studies which suggest that belonging is premised on a long period of residing in a particular area with an established population (see Elias and Scotson, 1994; Crow et al, 2002). Investing in social networks or neighbourly behaviour does not need to embody 'compulsory solidarity', based on a reaction to shared suffering (Crow, et al, 2002). These retired British women living on urbanisations in the Costa Blanca construct (or not) belonging to social networks to fulfil their common need for 'community'. In this way, although these women are not a persecuted minority, belonging to networks – or with quest companions – can be construed not so much as a survival strategy (Sherlock, 2002) but as a strategy to thrive in their new environment (see also O'Reilly, 2000a). This type of network community formation then, can be described as 'voluntary camaraderie', and reflects women's age, class, gender and ethnic positionalities: women '[draw] on their backgrounds in their choice of friends and acquaintances' (O'Reilly, 2000a, 131). However, networks can also be circumscribed by social locations as I explain. Those women who wished to remain in Spain minimised any difficulties relating to social contact there, positioning themselves as overcoming obstacles through their agency, while those who planned to leave cast themselves as casualties of forces beyond their control.

As I have already explained, within the tourist space which women occupied in the Costa Blanca, there were numerous British-run bars, pubs and cafes which they frequented; indeed, I met the women numerous times in the 'Shamrock Club' or in an English bar without a name but known as 'Jilly's'.[1, 2] Many of the women talked about their social life in Spain being far superior to that in the UK: they had more time to have social contact with others because they were retired and there was a greater pool of (other retired) people with whom to socialise; and in Spain social circles were far less fixed and more fluid. In the excerpt below Agatha talks about how socially orientated life in Spain is, in four different ways:

> 'Well now, we've really found we know lots of people here (1)…this is more of a social (2), you know, everyday sort of thing…we go out quite a lot (3)…we do more socialising here (4), I think.' (Agatha)

By her use of 'we' Agatha presents her social life as shared with her husband. Similarly, Lillian talked about engaging in social activities with her partner, presenting this as 'the norm':

> 'We spend a lot of time with our friends, Win and Tom, and another couple, friends of theirs, Stella and Jim, from near to where we lived in England actually, so we sort of knew them although we hadn't actually met them, if you like.' (Lillian)

Lillian was friends with Win in the UK; they met at a playgroup when their children were very young, so had a long-standing friendship. Although Lillian and her husband did not know Win and Tom's friends from the UK before moving to Spain, the fact that they were from the same place made them more familiar than people they met once there and more likely to be 'like them', as the extract from her narrative illustrates.

Mabel and Myra, on the other hand, moved to Spain alone, and perhaps had a more pressing need for social contact than Lillian. Both Mabel and Myra were also very positive about the opportunities they had to socialise and meet other women in similar circumstances:

'I have made more friends since I came to Spain than I made in all the 20 years I lived in [south coast of England], and I've only been here one year.' (Mabel)

'Well me and Joan and Mabel and Margot go out together quite a bit. There's another two ladies, Nelly and Marie, who are on their own who sometimes come too.' (Myra)

For some women, however, increased social contact could be a challenge (see Ahmed, 2012). For example, Olive acknowledges that although it is easy to make friends, eventually this can become intrusive:

'It's easy to make friends but after a while...you just want to push them away, and cut them off.' (Olive)

Through her metaphorical use of 'push them away' and 'cut them off', Olive narratively constructs boundaries between herself and others. Like Olive, Joy is ambivalent about Spain, yet does not want to return to the UK. Joy's feelings about her compatriots however, are unequivocal and she constructs boundaries predicated on distinction:

'We'd seen what there was. We'd met so many people and obviously we'd ferreted out the dross of humanity that we didn't want to make permanent friends of.' (Joy)

Although Joy does not define herself and others in relation to class, examining the linguistic devices she uses in her narrative account allows me to 'look at the defensiveness and the unstated in [her] views on class and to carefully read behind what is said' (Savage et al, 2001, 878). The literal meaning of 'dross' is the scum that forms on molten metal as a result of oxidisation, but its metaphorical meaning here, applies to people who are worthless and base, and certainly not 'like them'. From the excerpt of Joy's narrative, it seems that constructions of class positions are evidenced through habits, tastes and personal relations (Oliver and O'Reilly, 2010). Class is also apparent in relation to the ladies' club, as I discuss later in this chapter.

For some women, social contact and networks in Spain are not as meaningful as those left behind in the UK (O'Reilly, 2000b); this tended to be a theme in the narratives of those women who want to return to the UK or are ambivalent about remaining in Spain. Both Olive and Deidre felt that although there were more opportunities to meet new people in Spain, the depth of these friendships did not compare with those they had in the UK:

'I say I've got a lot of friends, but it's not quite the same as friends I had in England, not here.' (Olive)

'We've met lots of people here, but the people that we have back in England are still I would say, personally, we feel, or I feel deep for.' (Deidre)

For Joy and Enid, true friendships are based on longevity which precludes those associations made in Spain:

'I believe friends are the people with whom you share a past.' (Joy)

For Enid too, social networks 'at home' in Northern Ireland were with other married couples, or people like her and her husband:

'Well in Northern Ireland we have friends that we've had all our lives since we got married; a small number I would say, you know husband and wife, and maybe about six or seven couples, but friends we've known forever.' (Enid)

Spending time with partners: an obstacle to overcome?

An issue raised by several women was the amount of time that they found themselves spending with their partners. Earlier in their talk, Agatha, Lillian and Joy established that they spend social time with their husbands and other couples (people like them) and for them, this was not expressed in terms of being problematic. Also, Both Bernice and Agnes seemed to welcome the opportunity to spend more time with their husbands, evidenced by the following extracts from their narratives:

'Here it's funny but when we go out we're always both together, and he won't, he hates shopping at home, we never go shopping together at home, and here we go together.' (Bernice)

'[In Spain it's] a lot better [than in the UK], a lot more quality time with each other which at home we didn't have, you see.' (Agatha)

For Bernice and Agatha spending an increased amount of time with their partner can be construed as a positive change, but for Celia and Cynthia it became clear that this was a challenge and an obstacle that needed to be overcome:

'The biggest problem with moving abroad…was spending 24 hours a day with your husband, without being unkind.' (Cynthia)

Cynthia does not want to be perceived as being derogatory about her husband, or to cast herself as a 'bad' wife; and this fits with how she previous narratively positioned herself in relation to decision-making in migration (see Chapter Four). Her use of 'without being unkind' signals how she wants to be heard by the audience. Celia struggles to establish narrative footing (Gubrium and Holstein, 1998) demonstrated by her faltering use three times of 'I would say', 'I've got to say', 'I say'. Like Cynthia, she does not want to situate herself as transgressing norms of what a good wife is and since she wants to present a positive account of her migration decision and experience (Torkington, 2012) she narratively minimises the impact of 'living with a partner 24 hours a day' by a comparison to what retirement in the UK would be like:

'I would say, I've got to say, the hardest part, I say, is coming and living with a partner 24 hours a day. I've not been used to that, but if you're retired in the UK you'd have exactly the same, that's for sure.' (Celia)

Celia asserts independence and exercises agency by purchasing a 'little car' so that she is not reliant on her husband. In the following excerpt from her narrative, obliquely recounting an exchange they had, she positions herself as having agency, by saying 'I am not one that wants to be driven to the shops', although her use of 'little' three times in relation to the car diminishes any potential threat posed by her need for independence:

'So I said [to my husband] "I need to have a little car here, and I need to be independent. I was independent in England." So I got myself a little car, so I can get in the car,

go, do my own thing which is for me, great. I'm not one
that wants to be driven to the shops, doing this and that,
so I got the little car.' (Celia)

Jenny on the other hand is thwarted by her apparent dependence
on her husband. She begins by explaining that 'We're not ones for
travelling around', but further into this section of her talk it becomes
evident that it is in fact her husband who is unwilling to venture out
of the urbanisation. Jenny says several times here that she feels impeded
by her husband's lack of interest in seeing more of Spain. As in the
decision to migrate to Spain, Jenny casts herself as passive and this
further prevents her from enjoying her life in Spain. As a result, for
her, 'the experience of being in the alien world becomes less and less
pleasant (Booker, 2004, 98):

> 'We're not ones for travelling around. [Husband] doesn't
> like travelling and really we haven't seen parts of Spain that
> I would like to see. He's quite content to stay at home and
> sunbathe and you…get in a rut and boredom sets in and
> now it's just part of your life. So, I think, really, we ought
> to get out and see a bit of Spain now we're here, but I
> wouldn't like to do it on my own.' (Jenny)

The ladies' club

Social as well as economic capital is an important factor in determining
people's ability to migrate (De Haas, 2010) and also profoundly
shapes their post-migration experiences. Social capital, representing
the resources that women have or have access to (Bourdieu, 1986;
Coleman, 1990; Putnam, 2000) is not value-free however, and does
not take account of gender (Edwards et al, 2003; Zontini, 2004;
Franklin, 2004) yet gender influences the kind of social networks
women construct while in Spain. The Silver Ladies club is an example
of what Karen O'Reilly (2000a) describes as the creation of symbolic
boundaries on the margins of Spanish society, constructed through
membership of British-run social clubs. Significantly too, the Silver
Ladies club provides an opportunity to consider gendered lifestyle
gatherings, since the social space that men and women occupy is often
separate (Lundstrom, 2014).

   As I mentioned in the introduction, Cynthia and Celia were
instrumental in setting up the Silver Ladies, a club which meets
fortnightly at the 'Shamrock Club'. It is exclusively British[3] and

attended by retired women. Both Cynthia and Celia suggest that its main purpose is both to provide married women with some social respite from their husbands and also to give women who have migrated alone the opportunity to enjoy social contact with other women:

> 'We decided we'd start a ladies' club; [it] gives ladies a couple of hours. Also, we didn't think about it at the time, but we have found that there's a lot of ladies here on their own where their husbands have died, or whatever, since they've come out here and so they're looking for something because it's very hard again. You don't want to go out with couples because you feel a gooseberry, so it's somewhere for them to go for a couple of hours. We have trips out, different things, so that takes up a lot of my time.' (Cynthia)

Celia's use of 'people need to come' (to the Silver Ladies) provides justification for her going there and her use of the words 'get released' below suggests constraint and that she feels trapped by spending too much time with her own partner. Using the term 'loved ones' softens what could be perceived as a negative sentiment. At the end of this section of talk Celia provides clues as to how she wants to be understood, she does not want it to be read that she is being negative towards her husband:

> 'People need to come and get released from being with their loved ones…You come here and you're retired, it's totally different, so I felt I needed, I didn't want to be with him, that sounds, I don't mean that to sound.' (Celia)

Cynthia presents the ladies' club as a survival strategy (Sherlock, 2002) and as a means to overcome the obstacle of spending too much time with partners:

> 'Everybody that you talk to has got this problem because they're spending too much time with their husbands because you're not working. So you've got no conversation, so you both need to have your own space. You both need to go and do something individually, so you've got other friends than each other, and you've got a different conversation so hence the ladies' club.' (Cynthia)

Celia talks about the ladies' club giving retired women in Spain the opportunity to spend time away from their husbands, and presents this as a commonly held reason, rather than hers alone:

> 'I think that's why a lot of ladies come to the club, just for the break to get away from the partner.' (Celia)

Typically, at the Silver Ladies' meetings there would be guest speakers, quizzes, games of bingo and raffles. Cynthia and Celia also organised trips out to local markets, and to Benidorm and Alicante for Christmas shopping; there were also social evenings, often based on British cultural practices from the past rather than the present (see also King et al, 2000; Oliver, 2008). The extract from Celia's narrative illustrates the influence of nostalgia and an orientation to the past and also the influence of cultural capital and positionality:

> 'We're doing a sort of old time music hall tomorrow night, and we'll have pie and peas like we northerners do.' (Celia)

When Celia talks about the reasons for setting up the Silver Ladies she again casts herself as having agency:

> 'I knew when I came out here I've not to sit back. It's not going to come to me here. I've got to come out here and do something about it, which I suppose starting [the ladies' club] was my way of trying to make a start and get into it, and that's it. It's wonderful really.' (Celia)

The Silver Ladies was popular and all but two of the women featured regularly attended the weekly meetings, however, it was seen by some as embodying something low about British culture and to be avoided. As Savage et al (2001) argue: 'Class does not determine identity, but it is not irrelevant either. It is a resource, a device, with which to construct identity' (2001, 888) and this is illustrated by the excerpts from Joy and Lillian's narratives:

> 'The people who go to [the Silver Ladies club] are not my kind of people.' (Joy)

> 'I don't like [the Silver Ladies], it's not me.' (Lillian)

It is often difficult to coherently express class because of its power (Bourdieu, 1984) and it is also sometimes problematic to acknowledge one's class (Skeggs, 1997), but both Lillian and Joy allude to class distinction through their use of 'not my kind of people' and 'it's not me'. It is evident here, too, that class is not straightforward or homogenous, and it captures more than occupational status and employment; it also involves social and cultural capital, tastes, lifestyle and world view (Bourdieu, 1984).

Since these women construct networks and belonging around lifestyle gatherings and a social rather than collective social action, it is apposite to refer to 'club capital' rather than social capital (Winter, 2000; see also Ahmed, 2012). Women's networks in the Costa Blanca are characterised by a lack of obligation (Sherlock, 2002; Ahmed, 2012), are lifestyle based (O'Reilly, 2000a), of 'limited reciprocity' (Crow et al, 2002, 137) and are often pragmatic and superficial (Ahmed, 2013). Women's capital and the relationships which they can have are also affected by social locations (Skeggs, 1997), or positionalities: so their social and cultural capital is shaped by their gender, age, ethnicity and class. In this way, social and cultural capital influences the kind of networks that women can belong to and also how they construct belonging. Social and cultural capital are also important in relation to language, as I now unravel.

The important role of language

Language as structure and agency plays an important role in constructing and reflecting the world, and the language that people speak can shape how they see themselves (Temple, 2008b) and other people. For the women in this study, only speaking the English language is shaped by their age and class and ethnic positionalities and simultaneously reconstitutes boundaries between 'them' and 'others'. Being unable to speak the host's language was an important factor discussed at length in all of the women's accounts.[4] All of the women conceded – usually somewhat guiltily – that they should be able to speak the language of the country in which they lived. Those women who wanted to stay in Spain presented their inability to speak Spanish as unfortunate but ultimately not detracting from their enjoyment of Spain. However, those who planned to return to the UK structured their accounts differently and presented this as yet another obstacle that they could not overcome. In their narratives, women positioned themselves as passive and thwarted by obstacles in their attempts to learn Spanish, or as victims of circumstances outside their control.

Women arrived in Spain full of good intentions to learn the language, yet found that they can live the lifestyle without actually mixing with their hosts (Smallwood, 2007). However, similar to the expected osmotic benefits to health by living in Spain, it was clear that many of these women hoped to acquire Spanish language skills by virtue of simply living there, as Joy's comment illustrates:

'Well, I certainly thought I would learn working Spanish.'
(Joy)

Later-life migrants cannot easily adapt to new languages and customs (Torres, 2004) and older migrants often have a low belief in their ability to learn a new language (Huber and O'Reilly, 2004). Many of the women attributed their reluctance to learn Spanish to their age, and women's limited cultural capital influenced their non-engagement with learning Spanish. Yet there are other factors which also contribute to this.

Cynthia identifies 'the problem' – British people not speaking Spanish – in structural terms: first due to the lack of Spanish people living nearby:

'The problem here is there's not enough Spanish [people]
in this particular area.' (Cynthia)

She also blames the education system in the UK for not equipping British people with the necessary skills to learn other languages:

'We don't have any language skills and this is the fault of
the education system in England.' (Cynthia)

While Vera prefigures other nationalities as having a greater aptitude to learn languages:

'The non-English, like the Germans and the Swedes and
the Norwegians [and] the Dutch seem to find it easier to
learn Spanish than we do because of the verbs.' (Vera)

Here, Vera positions being 'English'[5] as the norm and all other nationalities as other (see Skey, 2011), embodying ideas of 'us' and 'them' (O'Reilly, 2000a). This is evident in Bernice's narrative when she casts the Spanish population as having the responsibility for speaking English through her use of 'you can get by, they understand a bit of

English'. Here, 'you' are British migrants and 'they' are the Spanish, so boundaries are demarcated and reconstructed. Once outside tourist space however, 'nobody can speak any English':

> 'Most people round this area, you can get by, they understand a bit of English, but if you go out...stopping off in different places you know, it's really, really Spanish and nobody can speak any English.' (Bernice)

Celia seems to accept that she probably would not learn Spanish at this point, given the length of time she had already been in Spain. In this excerpt from her narrative she casts herself as passive which contrasts to other parts of her talk, so there is evidence of narrative slippage (Gubrium and Holstein, 1998) here. Celia focuses on the obstacles to learning Spanish and prefigures herself as someone thwarted by a system that she is unable to properly navigate. She also presents other characters in the story as putting obstacles in her way; first, Cynthia, someone who was presented as an authority, is described as deterring her on the grounds of age, since she was not yet 60 years old, and second, the language teacher, since only Spanish is spoken during the lessons. She uses supposition or hearsay nine times in the extract below:

> 'I do believe (1) that they have [Spanish lessons] at the Town Hall on certain days, but I think (2) you've to be over sixty...Now I've heard (3) a lot of people have been to that, but the problem is, I don't know (4), I'm just thinking (5), Cynthia said (6) there was a great demand and you've got to be over sixty. I think (7) the college in Torrevieja does Spanish lessons and you pay for those but I believe (8) that the teacher there doesn't speak English. Most people who go to these lessons – there might be 23 the first week in the class – then you hear (9) the last few that are going and they're down to four or five. You ask Cynthia, she'll put you straight with all that.' (Celia)

In the final part of her narrative Celia shifts the focus to the logistics involved in accessing Spanish lessons rather than her inability to speak Spanish.

Lillian, too, laments that she cannot speak the language, and also positions herself as passive and thwarted. Here she seems to imply that it is actually beyond her control but says self-consciously, in five different ways, that she feels uncomfortable about not being able to speak the language of her hosts:

> 'I wish I could speak the language (1)…I don't like not being able to converse (2), I feel ignorant (3) and I feel that because I live in someone else's country I should speak their language (4)…I feel embarrassed (5).' (Lillian)

However, although most women apologetically presented themselves as thwarted by obstacles, others appeared relieved that they did not have to learn Spanish since it was possible to speak only English in the areas in which they lived, as Margot's comment illustrates:

> 'Everyone around here speaks English, even the Spanish people in the shops…It's made us feel a bit more at home.' (Margot)

Constructing 'Englishness'

Throughout their narratives women referred to themselves as being 'English', rather than British, although this was not presented as an ethnic category as such. It is useful at this juncture to consider the significance of Britishness and Englishness as ethnic or national positionalities. Byrne (2007), in her study of white women in inner city London, refers to the contested and racialised nature of Englishness as a national identity, posing the important question: 'Where does Englishness stop and Britishness begin?' (2007, 509). There were many different ways of representing Englishness in the women's narratives, most commonly derived from prefiguring 'Englishness' as the norm and all other nationalities and ethnicities – immigrants to the UK as discussed in Chapter Four, and Spanish people in this chapter – as 'other'. Women construct boundary markers centring on two aspects of Wright's (1985) depictions of 'Englishness': 'deep Englishness', denoting an idealised attachment to a rural idyll as discussed in the previous chapter; and second, 'empty Englishness' which is 'a sense of Englishness that is closed, fixed and white' (Wright, 1985, 522). Although uncertainty often defines the demarcations between Englishness and Britishness (Cohen, 1982), Englishness can be understood as romantic and nostalgic imaginary; while Britishness represents the opposite of the idyll, urban and multi-racial (Byrne, 2007). In this way Englishness represents an orientation to the past and Britishness epitomises the present.

This is further illuminated in UK political and policy circles, where debates about Britishness centre on interpretations of belonging and non-belonging (Marsh et al, 2007). While the fieldwork was being conducted, the then Labour government emphasised the assimilation of plural minority ethnic groups in the hope of creating 'patriots of the future' (McGhee, 2005), with a focus on networks through bridging (WD40) rather than bonding (superglue) social capital (Putnam, 1993; Alibhai-Brown, 2007). Social capital (as developed by Putnam, 2000) was used extensively by the New Labour government as a cure-all for community ills: in the UK, minority ethnic groups were encourage to 'bond' less with their own communities and to 'bridge' with majority populations to create cohesive national communities. All aspects embody both real and imagined elements: for example, the outward demonstration of ethnic and national identity was exemplified by the Government's vision of a shared future which is that to be British is to have or at least to demonstrate belonging to the country as a place through citizenship ceremonies premised on old traditions. The Home Office conceptualised belonging to a national 'community' in positivistic, essentialist terms with directly measurable elements, for example, speaking English, swearing allegiance to the monarchy and bridging to other ethnic groups. Joy draws an interesting parallel with the 'general knowledge test in the UK' (citizenship test) and expectations placed on migrants to the UK, and to her ability to pass such a test in Spain. The British in Spain do not have to undergo such a test, nor is there any expectation by the Spanish government that they integrate with their hosts. Here, Joy says that she does not feel that she belongs in Spain in four different ways:

> 'I don't feel part of things (1)...I don't understand the culture (2) because of the lack of language. (3) I can't find out who's who (4). I would never be able to pass a general knowledge test...as is now being called for by foreigners living in UK.' (Joy)

The UK requirement that migrants speak English and adopt a 'British' way of life to gain citizenship can be understood as both symbolic and utilitarian (Alexander et al, 2007) and both imagined and real. Women who migrated to Spain were patriots of the past; they rejected the 'new order' and instead attempted to recreate – or regain – community and belonging elsewhere. In this way their nostalgic narratives of community and belonging in Spain can be understood as counter-narratives to the government's meta-narrative of fostering belonging to the UK (place) by different groups bridging across social networks and by restoring Britishness. As discussed previously, counter-narratives are 'The stories which people tell and live and which offer resistance, either implicitly or explicitly, to dominant cultural narratives' (Andrews, 2004, 1). Women achieved this resistance through a narrative orientation to the past and nostalgic constructions of Englishness. This suggests that Britishness is inclusive and Englishness is exclusive and by referring to England and claiming Englishness, women appear to reject Britain, what 'Britishness' represents and in this way also modernity, since: 'Englishness is somehow truly what England should be...while Britishness is a category which can absorb all that disturbs this nation' (Byrne, 2007, 518).

Most women made distinctions between themselves and immigrants to the UK (particularly in terms of their presence not being detrimental to their host). However, there are parallels with the British retirees' situation in Spain with newly arrived immigrants to the UK. Since they cannot speak the indigenous language they are excluded from mainstream society and find themselves living a ghettoised life in the host country. Clearly, though, they are not financially disadvantaged in relation to the Spanish nor is the status of their ethnicity and culture perceived as inferior. However, there are symbolic (O'Reilly, 2000a, 2000b), constructed and 'real' boundaries as a result.

As I explained in Chapter Four, Cynthia, in particular, had strong negative views towards immigrants to the UK, yet here she talks about British immigration to Spain as unproblematic to their Spanish hosts. Through her use of banal statements such as – 'We haven't come to Spain to take off the Spanish' and 'that's why they don't resent us' – represented as common sense or unworthy of comment, she shows a 'reciprocity of perspective' (Brown and Yule, 1983, 11; cited in Skey, 2011) denoting the assumption that people with whom she interacts (and possibly me as the audience) will share the same experiences and world view as her. Again, she appears to be speaking for all people in the same situation, using the collective pronoun 'we'. The assertion that British people are not taking anything from the Spanish has parallels with her earlier comments about how immigrants to the UK are a drain on the system and she prefigures herself and others who moved to Spain as independent. Cynthia's positive take on migration to Spain is shaped by the fact that she was staying in Spain and wants to tell a positive story about living there. Here, too, she homogenises the Spanish; she had no evidence that Spanish people did not resent northern European migrants to Spain – in fact reports in local newspapers at the time suggested that some did:

'We haven't come to Spain to take off the Spanish and this is why they don't resent us.' (Cynthia)

Myra, who also cited immigration to the UK as problematic, echoes Cynthia's views about the British in Spain:

'I feel we're putting money into their country so it's making this area richer than what it was, so we are feeding our money into their economy.' (Myra)

While Margot, on the other hand acknowledges that the British presence in Spain might not be so welcome:

'We've took over Spain a bit. You know, Spanish people mustn't be very pleased us all living in these lovely apartments and houses, and they're living in sort of, you know, not as nice as areas as we are.' (Margot)

Although in the main being English and speaking the English language was presented as the norm, Cynthia and Mabel both recognised that while not in the UK they were themselves in another's country and therefore 'foreign'; in this way identifying themselves as 'the outsiders':

'You're in their country, we should learn their language.' (Cynthia)

'We are the immigrants, we are the foreigners and you have to remember that.' (Mabel)

At other junctures in their talk, women described immigrants to the UK as sharing certain characteristics with themselves and so blurred the boundaries between 'us' and 'them'. Cynthia acknowledged that the way that migrants from the UK lived in Spain was not dissimilar to how migrants to the UK had settled – in their own communities – without integrating with their hosts. She uses 'we' to acknowledge that she had 'complained' earlier in her talk and made a distinction between the English – and her identification was English – and British when she talked about migrants forming their own communities, perhaps in order to disassociate herself from this view and diffuse responsibility:

'The very thing we complain about in England is happening here where the British people, we said British, not English,

are forming their own communities and not integrating as
they should because of the language. Language is the key.'
(Cynthia)

The women in Spain were unable to assimilate with their hosts. They
lived on the margins of Spanish society which maintained boundaries,
and there are parallels here to migrants in the UK. Migrants from the
UK to Spain homogenised the Spanish and this banal nationalism
(Billig, 1995) was imbued with a sense of superiority. This links
to Anderson's (1983; 2006) first paradox of the imagined political
community, that although the nation is a new construction there is a
subjective belief in its long history. This had an impact on migrants to
Spain and was used pragmatically in their construction of themselves
as patriots of the past.

Floya Anthias (2008) suggests alternative terms to understand
ethnicity as a positionality in the context of transnational belonging
through migration: hybridity, cosmopolitanism and diaspora. Hybridity
captures the 'pick and mix' of different cultures characterising
transnational practices while cosmopolitanism refers to sophisticated
ways of belonging to political and cultural communities across borders.
Neither of these terms is particularly useful to explain retired British
women's experiences in Spain, since both terms suggest a significant
degree of interaction and engagement with the host population and
country. The term diaspora (see Davidson and Kuah-Pearce, 2008;
Dudrah, 2004), can be understood as fluid identity formation and
refers to the experiences of migrants and indigenous populations and
their relationships with their country of origin. However, conceptually,
diaspora still privileges the central role of ethnicity in defining identity
(Anthias, 1998a) and can silence particular voices – usually women –
within a group (Temple, 1999). I find diaspora is useful to conceptualise
the processes involved in being from one place and of another and
also in terms of 'diaspora space' (Brah, 1996): women in Spain live in
particular locations remote from their hosts and this has an impact on
the construction and experience of their ethnic positionalities.

Living an English life in Spain: an obstacle or asset?

It became evident in Chapter Five that most of the women were
surprised and disappointed not to be living a more Spanish life in their
retirement; and key to this was the lack of Spanish people living in the
urbanisations. Those women who planned to stay in Spain managed

this dissatisfaction and focused on the opportunities to form networks with their compatriots, as Celia's comment illustrates:

'Well, it is a shame, we know no Spanish people, really, and I really thought we would, but I can't complain, I've met so many people out here. They do tend to come from England though.' (Celia)

Lillian also expresses disappointment at not forming friendships with Spanish people, but again is compensated by social contact with people from the UK:

'I thought, well hoped that we'd be making some Spanish friends, but there aren't any Spanish people round here, but we've got our friends from England here, haven't we, so we're ok.' (Lillian)

Cynthia could speak Spanish and presents herself here as keen to engage with Spanish people, although the subtext in this excerpt from her narrative is that there are limited opportunities to interact due to living on the urbanisation:

'I mix with anybody. I try as much as possible to speak to the Spanish if I can, but Spanish people tend not to live round here.' (Cynthia)

Those women who planned to return to the UK presented the lack of contact with Spanish people as another obstacle that could not be overcome, as Agnes and Enid's comments suggest:

'We really hoped we would live a Spanish life…[have] Spanish friends and so on. Instead I've ended up living an English life in Spain and it's not what I wanted, really.' (Agnes)

'Well, I thought we'd be going to nice Spanish restaurants and meeting Spanish people and it's not worked out like that at all.' (Enid)

Some women on the other hand, enjoyed being surrounded by compatriots and in an 'English environment'. Myra celebrates the fact that she was among 'English people', and chose this particular area because of the large English population. Myra narratively edits (Gubrium and Holstein, 1998) her account; she begins to talk about choosing where she lives because 'there were low' and then stops abruptly, and then shifts to saying 'mainly English people'. Her use of narrative editing could be to save face (Goffman, 1959); she may have been about to say Spanish or foreign people, but did not want to present herself in this way or she could have been influenced by her interpretation of my positionalities as the researcher or audience:

> 'Oh, it's England in Spain here, it really is. I love it. Like I said, I chose to live round here because there were low, er, mainly English people living here.' (Myra)

On not being English: Enid

Enid was keen to establish her 'otherness' from English people and raised the issue of feeling antipathy towards the English. As indicated earlier, she was from Northern Ireland and identified herself as Irish rather than British. Her dislike was partly as a result of her experience on the committee of her urbanisation and her negative experiences with her English neighbours. Although told with humour, Enid expressed some very strong views about how she felt. In so doing, she homogenised English people:

> 'Some of the English who are living in this urbanisation are horrendous; they really, really are. They've gathered the worst of the English; maybe they've thrown them out of England and put them here. I prefer the Germans to the English and that's saying something.' (Enid)

Enid was disillusioned with Spain and planned to sell her holiday home there. She reflects on why people seem to gravitate towards those with similar cultural values, using her experiences in Northern Ireland to illustrate her point. The extract below was prefixed by her saying that she was not happy about not living a Spanish life, although she concedes that people are probably more comfortable and at home with 'their own kind'. She suggests here that place of birth is probably the overriding factor shaping belonging and community and also for shaping identity. When Enid continues she asserts that the Irish and the English are very different – with the implication that the Irish are 'nicer' – but she makes several concessions. In her narrative, she frames this as her opinion rather than fact, saying 'I think' five times, and also implies that those people to whom she refers are not representative of all English people. She relates to me as someone who was not English, like her, posing rhetorical questions, 'Do you think so?', 'So you know what I mean?', and talks of 'the English' as though they are something that we are both not:

> 'I think, I even think that we're considerably different to the English, you know...do you think so? I think it's also because people who were born and brought up in the same area have more in common. Do you know what I mean? I think I'll always have more in common with people from Northern Ireland than anybody else. I think I will. I mean, they say they say there's a religious divide over there, but I've always said I'm a Protestant, but even Catholic people from Northern Ireland will, well people we know anyway, will say they have more in common with Protestant people in Northern Ireland, than with people in the south, even though they are the same religion, because it's the way they've been brought up and your values. You know how your whole life is formed is similar, so you come out here and get people from all sorts of backgrounds and all sorts of nationalities, so we're not going to have as much in common.' (Enid)

Othering the Spanish

> 'The Spaniards are so laid back and they don't care.' (Mabel)

> 'I feel like one of them.' (Phyllis)

UK migrants in Spain have minimal contact with their hosts and tend to homogenise them as foreign and 'other' in the main, and even positive comments about Spanish people are imbued with superiority (see also King et al, 2000). Although she does not know any Spanish people, early on in her narrative Phyllis talks about her perceptions of 'them', basing this on superficial impressions, 'They always look so nice', and compares Spanish people favourably to 'other others', in this case 'refugees' in the UK:

> 'I find the Spanish people very nice...They always look so nice and I rate them very, very highly, I really do, compared to our, you know, refugees in England.' (Phyllis)

Mabel has an almost missionary approach to the presence of the British in Spain, in terms of how imported cultural practices potentially have a civilising effect on Spanish people, although she acknowledges how she positions herself as superior:

> 'I think that we're going to teach them a little bit of this and that, and I'm sorry if that sounds arrogant, particularly with my great love, animals. Already the Spaniards are starting up their own animal sanctuaries and, miracle of miracles, they're starting gardening, getting rid of all the debris in their gardens. We have introduced something that is an institution in England: garden centres.' (Mabel)

Other women imbue Spanish people and construct Spanishness with what can be interpreted as a range of (contested) characteristics and emotions (Skey, 2011), or a *homo nationalis* (Wodak et al, 1994, 4, cited in Skey, 2011), as Mabel, Agnes, Vera and Myra's comments below suggest:

> 'It's a kind of love the Spaniards have, the *los niños* [the children] and for old people. It's an innate thing…but you get lovely laid back, sunny-natured Spaniards, particularly the men, they get into a car and they immediately grow two horns and a tail, they can't help it.' (Mabel)

> 'I always thought the Spanish were horrible with dogs, but they love their dogs…They're mostly like we are in England and that was a shock.' (Agnes)

> 'The Spanish are really nice people. I think they're a kind people. I've always said that the Spanish are like the English used to be 40 years ago before we got Margaret Thatcher.' (Vera)

> 'Their attitude to animals isn't very good…They have got a very funny attitude towards animals…That is the thing that I don't like about Spain, it's their attitude towards animals, bullfighting. Yes, but I think it's wrong.' (Myra)

There can be dissonance between imaginings of integration and post-migration realities and this shapes migrants' identity-making practices (Benson, 2011b). The women in this study were not integrated with

Spanish people, although they had initially expected to be. Some altered their original expectations and were generally satisfied with the situation, while others did not particularly want to network with other Britons. These women live on the margins of Spanish society which maintains boundaries, and there are parallels here to immigrants in the UK.

Conclusion

As noted in Chapter Two, for the quest to be a success, the central character needs to be accompanied by 'quest companions' or others sharing the same goal (compare Ahmed, 2013). However, although these women have a common aim of finding belonging and community, the plot of their narratives diverge in relation to the end point of plot movement, or the ending embedded in the plot (Bakhtin, 1981; Czarniawska, 2004): for some this is managed in Spain, while for others, certain obstacles became increasingly impossible to overcome. A further complexity here is how the women present their status as 'foreign', since many position the Spanish as the foreigners, even though they are the host population. In this sense being from the UK and speaking English are often positioned as an overarching norm, and are sometimes used to minimise the issues associated with not speaking Spanish. The women generally talked of immigrants to the UK as being unlike them; although a small number acknowledged that there were similarities and both constructions are apparent in the same accounts.

It seems that quest companions need to be 'people like us'. However, although this appears to be predicated on migrant status, shared country of origin and language, being from the UK and speaking English are not enough to guarantee belonging to social networks. Belonging to networks is shaped by and reinforced age, class, gender and ethnic positionalities and cultural practices. Retired migrants from the UK are a minority, not part of the mainstream, living parallel lives to their hosts in ghetto-like urbanisations. Speaking English also circumscribes the kinds of networks of which they could be part. For some, the recreation of England in Spain is something to be celebrated rather than presented as a problem. Boundary reconstruction in networks is therefore also premised on age, class, ethnicity and also on gender,[6] both in terms of identification and ascription. Beck (1992) suggests that individualism has diminished traditional established support with a potential consequence being that only temporary alliances are made. However, the transitory nature of network communities, however, need not be problematic since this type of 'cocoon community' (Korpela and Dervin, 2013) satisfies individual and group needs for belonging.

In the following chapter, the focus shifts to how women manage and negotiate family relationships in the UK, particularly with their children and grandchildren.

EIGHT

Renegotiating family relationships: managing intimacy from a distance

'There's quite a large number of people who go back to the UK, they don't settle. The main problem, number one, is the family; two, the husband drives them nuts.' (Cynthia)

Introduction

It is now becoming clear that the relationship between place – being from the UK and living in an urbanisation in Spain – shapes the kind of networks that women form and is also influenced by their translocated positionalities. For Cynthia, Celia, Mabel, Margot, Mabel, Agatha and Myra, fulfilling the quest's goal was possible because they were able to overcome a number of obstacles. Bernice and Viv were satisfied by living a heterolocal life, enjoying the best of both worlds, spending part of the year in the UK and part of the year in Spain, while Enid, disillusioned by the Costa Blanca, planned to find an alternative place in the sun. Deirdre, Agnes, Vera and Jenny found a number of obstacles insurmountable and wanted to return to the UK, although Jenny was thwarted by her husband's reluctance. Both Joy and Olive, although staying in Spain, were ambivalent about being there. Neither wanted to return to the UK, but life in Spain for them was far from idyllic. The previous chapter depicted women's life on the margins in Spain and drew some parallels with their pre-migration lives, presenting this as yet another obstacle to fulfilling the quest's goal of belonging and community.

In this chapter I focus on a final obstacle to women achieving a successful life in Spain, and perhaps this is the most important one: missing children and especially grandchildren[1] left behind. I explore how these different groups of women manage and negotiate family responsibilities in the UK and how location within gender, or in this case, being a grandmother – and to a lesser extent being a mother – is part of the migration experience (Ryan and Webster, 2008). I consider how women reconcile, reject and reconceptualise traditional notions of being a mother and grandmother once they have left the UK (Ackers, 2000; Ryan, 2004) and how this can sometimes be at odds with being a wife. It becomes clear that different migration trajectories and positions reflect conflicting feelings, perceptions and experiences. I begin by considering how theories of grandparenting styles and intergenerational solidarity are useful for my analysis before focusing on how Cynthia, Celia, Agatha, Mabel, Lillian, Myra, Margot, Olive and Jenny perform grandmother identities through their narrative accounts. I also explore how Vera and Joy manage remote relationships with family while away from the UK.[2]

Grandparenting styles and intergenerational solidarity

Although the primary focus of this chapter is on how women maintain positive grandmother identities while choosing to be away from the grandchildren, rather than 'styles' or 'types' of grandparenting, the work of Neugarten and Weinstein (1964) and Cherlin and Furstenberg (1985; 1992) is particularly useful for my analysis. Initially, Neugarten and Weinstein (1964) identified five types of grandparenting: first, formal, where there are clearly demarcated roles between parents and grandparents, with the parenting duty remaining with the parent; second, 'fun seekers', where grandparents are more like 'playmates'; third, distant figures, where there are only occasional meetings between grandparents and grandchildren; fourth, surrogate parents, where grandparents take on the role of parental responsibility; and fifth, reservoirs of family wisdom, where grandparents represent links with past and present generations. These five types were later distilled into three categories which are more commonly used (Sandel et al, 2006): formal, fun-seekers and distant figures. Neugarten and Weinstein's (1964) fun-seeker and distant-figure grandparent typologies are useful for my analysis since the women in this study construct positive grandmother identities by being 'fun-seekers' while also 'distant figures'. Drawing on these styles, Cherlin and Furstenberg (1985) typify the grandparenting relationship broadly in terms of intergenerational 'exchange' – denoting reciprocal giving and receiving of benefits – and 'influence' – referring to how grandparents represent authority figures. Within these two overarching categories there are five types of grandparenting, which are: detached; passive; influential; supportive; and authoritative. To summarise, detached and passive types of grandparenting can be understood in terms of being low on both exchange and influence categorisations. The detached style of grandparenting indicates very limited contact with grandchildren, whereas the passive style has more contact but minimal influence and limited exchange. Authoritative, supportive and influential grandparenting styles can be understood as being more active than the detached and passive types. Cherlin and Furstenberg (1985) characterise the authoritative style as high in terms of influence but low regarding exchange, with the supportive type being low in terms of influence and high regarding exchange. The influential type, as its name suggests, is high on both exchange and influence. However, intergenerational relationships are rarely so clearly bounded (Thang et al, 2011) and grandparenting styles change over time and need to be seen within the context of the lifecourse (Cherlin and Furstenberg, 1985).

Later, Cherlin and Furstenberg (1992) further revised these types into three categories of grandparenting styles: remote, companionate and involved. Through their narratives, I explore how retired women living in the Costa Blanca negotiate the conflict associated with being 'remote' or distant figures as a result of choosing to be away from their grandchildren, while also being a 'good' grandmother in terms of their involvement and influence with their grandchildren. Analysing the women's narratives in this way allows me to combine these categories in a manner which adds a further layer of complexity to women's construction of positive grandmother identities.

Banks' (2009) study of US retirement migration to Mexico is also useful for understanding how grandparents maintain positive identities and relationships with geographically distant grandchildren. Through thematic narrative analysis, Banks (2009) found that grandparents' relationships with their grandchildren are an important factor in relation to their identity. For example, although living in another country, and effectively relinquishing '[c]ommitment to a specific norm of family obligations' (Brannen, 2003, 5), Banks (2009) emphasises that love and attachment characterise intergenerational relationships and suggests that there can also be benefits to being 'away'. Further, developments in technology, for example, e-mail, texts and Skype, facilitate contact across space and between generations.[3]

Bengston's (1975; 2001) typology of intergenerational solidarity is also widely used in studies of intergenerational relationships (Ko, 2012) and is useful when attempting to understand how retired British women living in Spain, away from their grandchildren, narratively negotiate and construct their grandmother identities. Bengston (1975) identified six forms of solidarity: first, affectual solidarity, referring to the sentiments and evaluations family members express about their relationships with others; second, associational solidarity, denoting the type and frequency of contact between generations; third, consensual solidarity, relating to shared opinions and a particular world view; fourth, functional solidarity, relating to levels of intergenerational assistance; fifth, normative, solidarity, denoting expectations regarding filial and parental obligations; and finally structural solidarity, which relates to the opportunities for interaction between older and younger generations. What is important is that the six dimensions of intergenerational solidarity also encompass conflict. Bengston et al (2002) subsequently revised the model into the solidarity/conflict framework. In this model, each dimension of solidarity also intersects with conflict: 'Each of the multiple dimensions of solidarity is distinct (orthogonal) and each represents a dialectic: intimacy and distance (affectual solidarity), agreement and dissent (consensual solidarity), dependence and autonomy (functional solidarity), integration and isolation (associational solidarity), opportunities and barriers (structural solidarity), familism and individualism (normative solidarity)' (Bengston et al, 2002, 571).

The intersection of solidarity and conflict is also often characterised by ambivalence (Bengston et al, 2002), and grandparenting is often an ambivalent experience for many grandparents (May et al, 2012) since conflicting feelings and ideas characterise intergenerational relationships (Lüscher and Pillemar, 1998; Lüscher, 2000). May, Mason and Clarke (2012) identify 'being there' yet 'not interfering' as two norms affecting grandparents in western societies. 'Not interfering' means that grandparents should not discipline or parent their grandchildren and any involvement should be approved by the parents. In this way, 'not interfering' can be understood in terms of grandparents relinquishing their 'influence' on their grandchildren. 'Being there' on the other hand, represents the 'caring face' of not interfering (May et al, 2012, 145) and involves grandparents remaining in the background and providing support when needed. I suggest that 'being there' can also be understood in terms of grandparents being available for 'exchange' – emotional, practical and financial support – when required. May et al (2012) argue that the norms of 'being there' and 'not interfering' are both highly passive which also conflict with other norms of independence, agency and self-determination. In this way different generations can be caught up in tension; between on the one hand, reproduction of some aspects of family structures and on the other hand, innovation (Brannen, 2003). A structural narrative analytical approach allows for the examination of British migrant women's constructions of grandmother identities and explores how they manage and negotiate the ambivalence characterising these. Ambivalence is apparent in relation to the contradictions and paradoxes involved in these women exercising agency by moving to Spain in retirement and how they reconcile this choice with the normative expectation of grandmothers 'being there'.

Performing grandmother 'identities' through narrative analysis

The women featured narratively construct positive grandmother identities while living away from their grandchildren in Spain and negotiate the conflict associated with 'not being there' and being a 'good grandmother'. Each of the women's narratives brings something unique to understanding grandmothering from a distance, although there are also some common themes to emerge from their narratives as follows: how grandmothering changes across the lifecourse; reciprocal intergenerational love and attachment; reconciling geographical and emotional distance; negotiating individualism and familism; how autonomy – theirs and their grandchildren's – is managed; and how 'being there' is taking new forms. During their narratives, the length of time women focused on their grandmother identities varied, and the excerpts below reflect this.

Cynthia

Cynthia has eight grandchildren, ranging from ages 14 to 18 (all male) and all eight grandchildren live in the same locale where Cynthia and her husband did in the UK, although the oldest grandson is about to leave to join the army. Until she left the UK, Cynthia worked full time so was not involved in surrogate-parenting of her grandchildren, although she played an active role in their lives, particularly when they were very young when they stayed with her during school holidays. The way Cynthia positions herself as a grandmother is complex. When she begins to talk about the family she left behind in the UK, she has a false start, faltering in her narrative footing. It is clear that she is thinking through how to position herself and this allows herself time to establish a preferred identity as a geographically distant, but nevertheless loving grandmother who is attached to her grandchildren. However, since she chose to leave them behind in the UK she needs to present a plausible story to reconcile this paradox. Cynthia's normative talk acknowledges the meta-narrative or wider discourse of how a 'good grandmother' would feel in her circumstances and emphasises that this also applies to her:

> 'Well, how do I? How do I? I know everybody says you miss
> your children and you do, and you miss your grandchildren.'
> (Cynthia)

Cynthia presents herself as a sensible, no nonsense woman who is
pragmatic rather than emotional in the decision that she has made in
terms of moving to Spain. She casts herself as liberating her family – as
well as liberating herself – from obligation and duty and in this sense
she is able to be both a wise and generous grandmother. Cynthia's
account also highlights how intergenerational relationships change
over the life course (Cherlin and Furstenberg, 1985). The sub-text is
that her active and influential role as grandmother to young children
has ceased and her grandchildren have become more independent.
Cynthia narratively manages this changed relationship by emphasising
that grandmothers must, by her use of 'you've got to', encourage the
loosening of ties:

> 'Once, when they're children, it's lovely when they're very
> small, but as they get older they've got their own friends.
> You've got to let them go their own way.' (Cynthia)

In the next excerpt from Cynthia's narrative she continues the themes
of non-interference by saying 'you can't live their lives'. Not-interfering
is a normative expectation of 'good grandparenting', so by emphasising
this, as well as being freed from obligation towards her grandchildren,
Cynthia's positions herself in a positive manner. She also emphasises
that love and attachment characterise grandchildren's feelings towards
their grandparents by saying 'they still love you'. She uses the word
'wrench' to describe her feelings about moving to Spain and leaving
her grandchildren behind, suggesting almost physical pain at being
separated from them. Cynthia negotiates the tension between intimacy
and distance (Bengston et al, 2002) by minimising the significance
of the geographical distance between herself and her grandchildren
and emphasising that geographical distance is not synonymous with
emotional distance or lack of intimacy. She focuses on the opportunities
and de-emphasises the barriers to contact with her grandchildren,
which reinforces sustained family integration:

> 'With your grandchildren, you can't live their lives, so
> although it is a wrench and you've got to keep in touch
> with them, but you're not that far away and when they get

to a certain age, as much as they love you, and they still love you no matter what age.' (Cynthia)

Cynthia ends this part of her story by re-emphasising the need for her family to live their own lives and thus reinforces the norm of non-interference and also the loosening of intergenerational duty and obligation. The use of 'got to' in relation to 'do their own thing' and 'live their own life' is particularly emphatic and she uses this phrase twice. In this excerpt Cynthia focuses on the benefits of being away (Banks, 2009) saying that it is 'exciting' for her grandchildren to visit her in Spain and there is also an element of the 'fun-seeker' grandparenting style performed here. In this way, for Cynthia, the grandmother relationship does not seem to be characterised by duty or obligation, but instead, it is '[a] more light-hearted role' (Sandel et al, 2006, 267). Cynthia uniquely takes the non-interference principle to an extreme, focusing on how her move to Spain has granted her grandchildren freedom:

> 'They've got to do their own thing, and so, and I didn't want it to become a chore for them to come and visit grandma, whereas now it's exciting to come and to visit...They've got to live their own lives.' (Cynthia)

Celia

Celia has one granddaughter, aged three who is the child of her only child. Celia lived in the city where she was born until she moved to Spain. Her daughter left to go to university aged 18 and has lived several hundred miles away ever since. Before moving to Spain, Celia saw her daughter infrequently and casts herself as having adjusted to a limited role in her life since she has 'always lived away'. However, the arrival of her granddaughter, the year before she moved to Spain represented 'a pull', emphasised twice, denoting attachment, or ties that bind:

> 'The first grandchild, now that was a bit of a pull because that's the only thing, I think that when people my age come out here, grandchildren probably, maybe sons and daughters if they've lived near them, they're used to seeing them day in day out, but I wasn't. My daughter always lived away so it's my grandchild the pull was.' (Celia)

Celia hints at a lack of intimacy as well as geographical distance between herself and her daughter. Her isolation from her daughter is presented as something that Celia cannot control, and is habituated to. Her use again of "pull" in relation to her granddaughter re-emphasises her feelings of love and attachment and she minimises the physical distance between herself and her granddaughter, highlighting the ease with which she can travel to see her. Celia casts herself as someone who is comfortable with the (individualistic) choice to leave her granddaughter since it does not mean that she is isolated from her family (familism). She focuses on the opportunities for contact and minimises the barriers to visiting her granddaughter by comparing the travel logistics from Spain and her home city. A sub-text here is that although Celia is geographically remote from her granddaughter, this is no more remote than if she was still living in the UK and that this does not have an impact on any involvement with her:

> 'Yes, my daughter lives down in [south of England]…so I probably used to see her about every three months, three or four months, so I can live with that. It's my granddaughter, who's now three, that the pull is there. But saying that, if I lived down in [north-east England] and she still lived in [south of England] it would probably be the same distance, I can get on a flight from here and be in [UK airport] in two and a quarter hours, to go down the motorway from [south of England] is four, four-and-a-half hours, so it's about the same really by the time I've gone to the airport and that.' (Celia)

Celia was the only women in the study who talked about their children's response to the decision to migrate to Spain in retirement. She reported her daughter as saying 'Mum, go for it' when told about her parents considering the move. In this way, she presents her daughter as sanctioning the move to Spain and giving her permission to leave the UK.

Agatha

Prior to leaving the UK, Agatha lived in the same town where was born. Agatha was a stay at home mother to her own children until they were teenagers. She has five grandchildren aged from nine to thirteen. Three of her grandchildren – aged six, nine and ten – still live in her home town and before moving to Spain Agatha played an active role in their lives, looking after these children two days a week while her daughter went to work. Early in her narrative, when she began to talk about missing the family in the UK, Agatha emphasises the 'taken for granted' love and attachment characterising a grandmother's feelings towards her grandchildren by her use of the rhetorical, 'I'm a grandmother, aren't I?' She positions herself as a loving grandmother who must manage the pain associated with being separated from her grandchildren and suggests that this is more difficult for her than her husband, the grandfather. It is evident here that physical distance does not weaken strong feelings of emotional attachment:

> 'Oh yes…very much so, harder for me than for [husband] because I'm a grandmother, aren't I?…I still have pangs.' (Agatha)

Like Cynthia's 'wrench' and Celia's 'pull', Agatha's use of 'pangs' conveys the feelings of pain associated with a grandmother's separation from her grandchildren. For Agatha this can be understood in terms of the ongoing difficult feelings surrounding missing her grandchildren and relates to the conflicts experienced in terms of affectual, associational, structural and normative solidarity. I revisit this in the conclusion below. Agatha's comment 'I'm a grandmother, aren't I?' can also be understood as a form of 'normative talk', and normative talk is 'one of the ways in which individuals work out the "fit" between cultural norms and their own everyday experiences through the narratives they tell of their lives' (May et al, 2012, 140).

When Agatha's talk focused on the differences between her life in Spain and the UK, her role and involvement in her grandchildren's lives was presented as the most significant. Negotiating the separation from her grandchildren and the relinquishment of her care-giving role was clearly an ongoing issue for Agatha. She talked of her life in Spain in terms of increased leisure opportunities, for example, being able to go out more, but it was evident through her narrative that adjusting to the diminishment of her familial role and a more individualistic lifestyle was an on-going and difficult process. Agatha did not easily exchange the familial intimacy with her grandchildren for the freedom that being in Spain offered (O'Reilly, 2000b):

> 'The only difference is I probably wouldn't go out as much…I'd probably still be looking after my grandchildren because I'd just be the end of a telephone.' (Agatha)

Agatha frames the benefits to being away from home in terms of having more 'quality time' with her grandchildren when they visited and emphasises the frequency of contact when she says, 'They've all been this year'. There is conflict for Agatha in terms of being unable to perform the grandmother role which for her seems to entail physically being there despite what she says below. In her closing talk about her family she again focuses on the continued communication with her family in the UK and presents herself as a loving and involved grandmother despite being geographically distant:

> 'They've all been this year, so you get more quality time with [them] really. You don't realise that at home, you're just at the end of the telephone – "Mum can you do this?" I phone them up all the time.'

For Agatha, being a grandmother appears to involve being physically proximate to her grandchildren. Her previous exchange in terms of providing childcare support involved 'being there' and it is clear that she experiences ambivalence arising from not being in the UK. Agatha's ambivalence can therefore be understood to be gendered (May et al, 2012).

Mabel

Mabel was unusual in the sample of women interviewed in two important ways: first, at 83, she was significantly older than the other respondents; and second, at the age of 60, she and her husband became surrogate parents for their only grandchild when her son and his wife died in a car accident when the grandson was ten months old. In her narrative, Mabel shows how her role as grandmother has changed across the life-course of both herself and her grandson. From being highly involved in his early life and upbringing, when the time arrived that her grandson 'had grown to the point he could care for himself', Mabel then had the freedom to pursue her ambition 'to go abroad to live'. Her use of 'longings' and 'cravings' for 'another scene' suggests a strong desire for a different life; one where she can for the first time prioritise her wishes. There is a sense that Mabel is able to exert individualism in her decision to move to Spain and leave her grandson, since she had previously prioritised his needs. She casts herself as happy to relinquish responsibility as she had effectively discharged her duty. The principles of non-interference are also evident here, and appear to be endorsed by both Mabel and her grandson (Thang et al, 2011):

'I had a 10-month-old baby...and we brought him up and I think we had a fair amount of fun one way or another... You might well ask why did these longings start in me, cravings to have another scene, can I start now on the reasons why I decided to move, to, to leave? My husband died in...1990 and as soon as my grandson had grown to the point he could care for himself, be independent, which is what young people like, I decided that I wanted to go abroad, to live.' (Mabel)

Mabel's narrative suggests that she does not want to curtail her grandson's ability to 'be independent'. Equally, however, she is clear about exercising her own freedom and individualism to fulfil her desire to 'have another scene'. Mabel had been more involved in the upbringing of her grandson than any of the other women in the study, for her the boundaries between 'not interfering' and being involved in her grandson's life were blurred since she assumed responsibility for his upbringing in the absence of his parents. In this way, Mabel's duty towards her family has been discharged and her ambivalence regarding her grandmother identity is minimal. Further, Mabel's grandson is her only remaining family:

'My family are either deceased or I've lost contact with them, and I should say that I only had half a family: my mother was orthodox Jewish and they said "Shiva" because she married out...so I never met any of them...It's quite definite, I mean there's no going back, I bet you know about that.' (Mabel)

Here Mabel positions me as someone who would understand 'otherness' in terms of the dynamics involved in her family situation, either because of my education background or my own experiences.

Myra

Before moving to Spain, Myra lived in the same locale as her daughter and granddaughter and saw them both regularly and fairly frequently, as they came to visit every fortnight or so. Myra was not involved in any care-giving for her granddaughter; although she occasionally looked after her if her daughter went out in the evening. Myra acknowledges that it was her choice to come to Spain, she 'left', acting on an individual rather than familial premise, and minimises any difficulties in being separated, although concedes that she misses her granddaughter in particular:

> 'I left my daughter and my granddaughter and she's only 18 months, so, yes, I do miss her, but I will sort of be with them at Christmas and then I'll be back in the UK again next summer.' (Myra)

Again, Myra focuses on love and attachment and not on duty or obligation.

Margot

I mentioned in Chapter Four that Margot had looked after her father until his death before moving to Spain, so in a sense felt that she had discharged her daughterly duties towards him. Margot had two daughters and a son and only one daughter lived close to where she lived in the UK. Margot had been involved in caregiving for her granddaughter, aged five, and both her granddaughter and daughter had lived with her while her daughter was at university, and again this could be understood as Margot fulfilling responsibilities towards her granddaughter. Margot, like Myra focuses on the opportunities for seeing her children and granddaughter the following summer rather than on actively missing them; although there is no urgency, she hopes to see them all then. The fact that her other daughter and son live away also grants her freedom:

> 'One of my daughters lived with me for a while; I was looking after the granddaughter while she did her degree. My son lives in Australia with his Australian girlfriend and my other daughter lives in London. But I hope to sort of catch up with them all when I'm home in the summer holidays, see them all then.' (Margot)

Lillian

Lillian has three sons, the eldest is married with three children aged six to ten, while the younger two are both single. They all live within a 100-mile radius from where she lived in the UK. Although Lillian and her husband usually saw their sons on Sundays, she was not involved in any caregiving for her grandchildren. Her son's mother-in-law looks after the grandchildren for two days a week when her daughter-in-law goes to work part time. Her eldest son and daughter-in-law plan to buy a holiday home close to Lillian and her husband the following year and visit during the school holidays. Lillian acknowledges that she misses her family, particularly on Sundays, which she describes as 'family day'. However, she emphasises adherence to the non-interference principle in that contact was always pre-arranged since she recognised that he sons 'had their own lives'. Lillian and her husband are strategic in managing separation from the children and grandchildren by ensuring that they have things planned to ensure they enjoy their time in Spain:

> 'Sundays are the worst day here because it's family day, so we always plan something for Sunday. We usually go out and about, or if it's nice we go to the beach…but we didn't live in anyone's pockets, so it's always arranged, where they'll come to see us, it wouldn't be like I'd be seeing them every day or anything like that.' (Lillian)

Olive

Olive has a son and a daughter who each have two children. They live quite close to where Olive lived in the UK with her ex-husband (and her ex-husband still lives in the marital home) in the north-west of England. Olive saw her children and grandchildren regularly in the UK and occasionally looked after her grandchildren. Like her feelings about living in Spain, Olive acknowledges her ambivalence about being away from her children and grandchildren by saying 'it's good and bad'. She misses them, but also welcomes the fact that she does not have to become too involved in their lives and she narratively manages the tensions between individualism and familism. After a long illness and traumatic divorce, Olive appears happy to enjoy the freedom that being in Spain allows and emphasises that she takes pleasure in having time for herself:

> 'It's good and bad being away from family. It's bad as I miss them, but if I went back to England and got involved with them too much it takes over. So it's good for me that my time is now for me.' (Olive)

Jenny

Jenny did not want to be in Spain. Her husband was keen to move and she only agreed to come because her daughter and partner originally planned to move over themselves. However, this now seemed unlikely and Jenny was desperate to return to the UK, although her husband was insistent that he would not. Since she moved to Spain, Jenny's daughter had a daughter of her own and this made being away from the UK all the more painful for her. While she was living in the UK she saw her daughter almost every day and wanted to be involved in her granddaughter's life. For Jenny, love and attachment for her daughter and granddaughter are inextricably bound up with physical proximity.

> 'Well, I saw my daughter all the time, I thought they [daughter and partner] were coming here to live…and then she had my granddaughter and now I'm itching to go back. [Husband] thinks it's because of my granddaughter, well, it is because of my granddaughter, but I wanted to go back even before she was born. I want to be near them both really.' (Jenny)

For Jenny, like Agatha, being a 'good' grandmother appears to be premised on being physically proximate to her granddaughter. Her use of 'itching' to go back conveys the physical discomfort Jenny experiences as a result of being away. She wants to be proximate to her daughter and granddaughter and she cannot present a positive mother or grandmother identity while geographically remote.

Negotiating relationships

Both Vera and Joy did not have grandchildren but still needed to negotiate family responsibilities in the UK. Vera wished to return to the UK, and presented family responsibility and missing her daughter as overriding reasons to return and ultimately as insurmountable obstacles to staying. As indicated earlier, this can be understood as a shift in plot, from the quest to the voyage and return. For Vera, the life-renewing goal had not been achieved in Spain since; in addition to other obstacles previously discussed, she could not overcome the obstacle of missing family. For Vera, being a mother was the primary reason she gave for wanting to return to England since she was unable to manage being separated from her daughter. She also expressed feelings of guilt for being absent when her niece 'could do with some assistance' in caring for her sister-in-law:

> 'I miss my daughter. I miss my family, my sister-in-law, she's very ill. My niece could do with some assistance really. It's

very hard for [niece]. Of the three daughters my brother had, there's only one left in this country. One died and one's in Australia, so it's very hard for [niece] really 'cos she's working full time and she has to see her mother every morning, every night, and at weekend...so there's quite a lot of pull, and friends...but my daughter is the main person.' (Vera)

Joy

Joy has twin sons aged 26, both living near London with their respective partners. Joy emphasised love and attachment by saying 'of course I love my children to bits' and was pragmatic about contact with them, returning to the UK every three months to see them:

'The children are both living in the south of England, and of course I love my children to bits. We go back to UK approximately every three months for about a fortnight's visit.' (Joy)

Conclusion

Women who migrate need to manage and negotiate family responsibilities in their country of origin (Ryan, 2004). Those women who wanted to remain in Spain told a story of successfully negotiating such responsibilities in order to fulfil the quest's goal of belonging and community in Spain. For Vera and Jenny, missing family and being unable to successfully manage separation represents an additional obstacle preventing the quest from being achieved. My analysis of the women's narratives first began by an examination of the thematic content; in other words, focusing on "what" women said about their experiences of being a mother and grandmother while away from their children and grandchildren. All of the women identified love and attachment between them and their children and grandchildren as a powerful factor in characterising and sustaining intergenerational relationships (Banks, 2009). Indeed, love and attachment appeared to be more significant than duty and obligation, apart from in the case of Vera. Often, the benefits of being away (Banks, 2009) were highlighted in terms of allowing greater freedom for both grandmothers and grandchildren and this also fits with the non-interference principle (Bates, 2009; Mann, 2006) associated with being a 'good grandmother'. Second, examining some of the linguistic devices (Czarniawska, 2004) employed in the women's narrative practice further illuminates their experiences of migration and being away from their grandchildren. The use of emotive language, for example: 'pull', 'wrench' 'pangs' and 'itching', evokes and conveys a deep sense of physical discomfort which is almost visceral. Examining language choices can be understood as illuminating 'how' women convey their experiences. Finally, examining the structure of the women's narratives in terms of positionalities (Gubrium and Holstein, 1998) allowed for a consideration of the 'who' of the narratives. Women's decision to migrate in retirement represents a departure from the care-giving and kinship-keeping roles traditionally associated with grandmotherhood and being a mother. The grandmothers demonstrated an awareness of this normative expectation of grandmothering, but still managed to cast themselves as 'good grandmothers' throughout their narratives.

Vera and Jenny wanted to return to the UK, and missing family was presented as an insurmountable obstacle to settling in Spain, particularly for Jenny following the birth of her granddaughter. However, those women who had chosen to move to Spain in retirement and wanted to remain there needed to tell a positive story about their life there and minimise any potential problems. Missing their grandchildren and managing the conflicts associated with being away from them was the largest barrier to having a happy life in Spain; reconciling individualism with familism was a challenge for these women. In this way, their grandmother identities are strategic and positional (Hall, 2000). When women talked of missing their families, this was told as something that was painful, needed negotiation but was bearable overall. However, there clearly were more challenges for Agatha who had young grandchildren, and who had previously had an active care-giving role. Regardless, however, these women positioned themselves as being good grandmothers in spite of not being with their children and grandchildren and emphasised reciprocal love and attachment rather than exchange and influence as characterising intergenerational relationships. In this way, duty and obligation are minimised. Although geographically remote, they do not present themselves as 'distant figures', and are able to renegotiate and construct new forms of exchange and influence in order to present positive grandmother identities.

Retired British women living in Spain narratively construct grandmother identities within the context of structural, demographic and cultural social change and their narratives also reflect and illuminate these contexts. These women had the opportunity to move abroad in retirement, through freedom of EU movement, increased affluence and shifting expectations of grandmothering. The women featured have effectively chosen to live away from their grandchildren and this challenges the normative expectation of grandparents 'being there' (Bengston et al, 2002). This decision presented a situation of difficulty or moral dilemma since women needed to maintain and renegotiate a positive grandmother identity while away. Through their narratives, women reconcile the paradox of *not* being there with being a good grandmother and construct and reflect new forms of grandparenting 'as the social and economic contexts of family relationships evolve' (Timonen and Arber, 2012, 1). Good grandmothering is also synonymous with not interfering (May et al, 2012) and individualisation fits with the non-interference expectation and the loosening of tradition and obligation (Thang et al, 2011). Further, the norm of non-interference can be used as a vehicle to free the older generation who are still able to maintain '[a] limited but valuable role in their grandchild's life' (Sandel et al, 2006, 267).

The women featured experienced ambivalence as a result of 'a conflict between normative expectations of what a grandparent "should" do and their own wish to determine their lives in an autonomous fashion' (May et al, 2012, 146). They exercised agency in moving to Spain in retirement, so for them the ambivalence that they were expressing was more about how they reconciled being a good grandmother when they had effectively rejected the normative expectations of what a grandparent should do. Since '[n]arratives are strategic, functional and purposeful' (Riessman, 2008, 8), through their narrative accounts, most of the women are able to manage the ambivalence associated with being remote and renegotiate what a good grandmother is when 'not there'. They narratively manage the dialectic associated with solidarity and conflict in several significant ways. First, by emphasising that intimacy is sustained – is not synonymous with – but transcends geographical distance. In this way, intimacy with grandchildren is presented as something that is not compromised by moving to Spain and the physical distance between them is minimised. Second, by privileging autonomy over dependency and emphasising the benefits (to their grandchildren) of their being away, they are able to reconcile such individualism with familial orientation. Third, by focusing on the opportunities rather than the barriers to maintaining contact and relationships, these grandmothers present themselves as sustaining integration within their families. Proximity and easy access to the UK coupled with telephone contact and frequent visits avoids isolation. Significantly, therefore, although retirees may be remote, they remain involved. Finally, women emphasise strong, reciprocal and enduring love and attachment for their children and grandchildren and this is central to constructing a positive mother and grandmother identity. In this way, it is possible to narratively construct a positive identity while managing the contradictions and tensions associated with 'being away'.

Having unravelled the final obstacle to achieving the good life in Spain, in the following chapter I focus on 'the end point of plot movement', or where and how women locate home and community.

NINE

Locating 'home' and community: the end point of plot movement

> In [the quest]…the story ends on a great renewal of life, centred on a new secure base, guaranteed into the future. (Booker, 2004, 83)

> The complete happy ending of the voyage and return story is simply that the hero returns to [her] familiar world transformed. (Booker, 2004, 102)

Introduction

Throughout this book we have followed women's migration journeys across space and time as they spanned and reconstituted boundaries. Beginning with their pre-migration lives – characterised for many by fractured belonging in the UK – upper and more proximate structures enabled and facilitated their agency in moving to Spain in retirement. We have also seen that women's positionalities and unique biographies are also significant in shaping migration choices, decision-making processes and their post-migration lives. I framed divergent migration trajectories in relation to two plot typologies: the quest and voyage and return. Those women who ultimately chose to remain in Spain can be said to have fulfilled the quest of belonging and community in a new home; while those for whom the quest is not successful, voyage and return to the UK, and reconfigure it as home. Women living 'betwixt and between' emphasise the positives of Spain and living heterolocally, but identify the UK as home (see also Huber and O'Reilly, 2004). Of course, depending on whether or not women wished to stay in Spain, certain aspects are emphasised or minimised in order to justify present actions and future intentions. However, irrespective of where they wished to be, all of the women wanted to tell a positive story about themselves and the choice they make in relation to 'home' and this is evidenced through their narratives. Those women who choose to stay in Spain yet do not construct it as home convey ambivalence in relation to belonging.

Although the women construct home in relation to place, locating 'home' is complex and multi-layered (Huber and O'Reilly, 2004; Ryan, 2004). 'Home' can also be shifting, pragmatic and contingent, and, for these women, place represents more than merely space. Huber and O'Reilly (2004) use the German *heimat*, premising that it captures more than the English word 'home'[1] and 'most usefully conveys the struggles inherent in the creation of home, community and a sense of belonging' (2004, 330) which are more than, yet related to, place. The Icelandic *heima*[2] similarly represents emotions and feelings of belonging which are rooted to, but nevertheless transcend, place; and its translation into English is being 'at home'. How and where and why women felt *heimat* or *heima* captures the processes of constructing belonging to different kinds of community and embodies places and people. Further, it is shaped by their positionalities, and, importantly, it provides the antidote to *heimweh*, or homesickness. Now I return to the women's individual biographies for a final time to unravel their depictions and constructions of home.

Spain as home

Phyllis, Lillian, Celia, Agatha, Margot, Myra, Cynthia and Mabel prefigure themselves as being 'at home' in Spain or Spain as representing home, illustrated by the following excerpts from their narratives. Phyllis previously talked about feeling unsafe and excluded from the UK. Phyllis' use of 'we've made this our home' suggests agency and pragmatism: she and her husband do not want to return to the UK. They are happy to be in Spain for the benefits of the climate and improved quality of life, and the presence of her closest family enhances this. Phyllis is pleased to be surrounded by her compatriots and although she 'rated the Spanish very highly', she is not disappointed not to be more integrated with her hosts. This short extract from Phyllis' narrative suggests that home can be pragmatically constructed in a place of one's choosing:

'Well we've made this our home now.' (Phyllis)

Lillian and her husband also planned to stay in Spain, enjoying the enhanced quality of life there. Lillian did not cast herself as an escapee from the UK or as feeling fractured belonging, instead she and her husband wanted to benefit from the climate and live a more relaxed life in their later years, and Spain represented a place where this was possible. Their move was based on long-standing visits to the area and previously owning a holiday home in the region, so familiarity was also a factor. Although Lillian was rather dismayed by the excessive development in the area and not keen to socialise with "other Brits" since she found many "arrogant and rude", she and her husband could overcome this obstacle since they had an established social network from the UK which made her feel 'at home':

> 'Win and Tom have made us feel so welcome and well, at home, really.' (Lillian)

In this way Spain provides the context for Lillian to achieve *heimat* with known others 'like her'. Lillian minimised her disappointment in living a British life in Spain and negotiated the conflict from being away from her children and grandchildren, helped by her middle son planning to buy a larger holiday home close by, in which the rest of the family could stay when they visited. Again, Lillian's narrative depicts Spain as somewhere where she and her husband have chosen to be their home:

> 'We're going to stay in Spain, we may move inland and keep this as a holiday home, but we're definitely staying.' (Lillian)

From the start of her narrative Celia prefigured herself as having agency.[3] Beginning with her pre-migration life, to the decision to migrate and her post-migration practices, Celia overcame a number of impediments to achieving the good life in Spain through her own volition. Establishing the ladies' club, purchasing the 'little car', maintaining her independence and able to manage being geographically remote from her granddaughter enabled Celia to feel 'at home' in Spain. Although she was regretful not to live a more Spanish life, being unable to speak the language and having no Spanish friends, Celia adjusted her initial expectations and presented herself and her life in Spain in very positive terms. Again, Celia's narrative suggests that home can be chosen and for her captures the spatial or contextual (this place) and temporal (now) dynamics involved in being at 'home':

> 'This is our life now, this is our home.' (Celia)

Agatha and her husband planned to remain in Spain and were happy living among other British people in the urbanisation. They enjoyed the climate and slower pace of life, although Agatha desperately missed her grandchildren and struggled to handle being a remote grandmother.

Agatha had not been back to the UK for a long period and mentions this almost casually here. Interestingly she does not say 'This is *our* home now.' The second part of this extract is anonymous and she distances herself from what she says, as though it logically follows that where one lives is where one's home is, suggesting emotional dissonance, whereas the first part of the narrative excerpt is specific to her, and personal:

> 'Oh, it'll be nearly two years since we went back to England; we've been four or five times…You know, when you go back its lovely, but this is your home now.' (Agatha)

There is evidence of narrative slippage (Gubrium and Holstein, 1998), in Agatha's account. She establishes that she and her husband are living permanently in Spain, through gaining *residencia*, yet then adds that her husband would never return 'home'. In these extracts from her narrative, both the UK and Spain are referred to as 'home' and the excerpt below also illuminates gendered dynamics and agency in decision making within her household. Home for Agatha is multiple: she lives in Spain but her attachment to the UK persists because her family are located there. Although Agatha presented herself as having agency and the initial decision to migrate to Spain as consensual, the decision to remain in Spain is attributed to her husband, suggesting compliance:

> 'We are permanent, we just got our *residencia*…We've no intentions, well [husband] would never go back home.' (Agatha)

Both Margot and Myra were relatively new to Spain and were the most unequivocally enthusiastic about living there. Neither of these women presented any apparent obstacles to fulfilling the quest in Spain: they were happy to speak English, live among compatriots and enjoy 'England in Spain'. Margot was relieved to escape the UK; she hated the weather and had also run into financial difficulties prior to selling her house there. Given that she had cared for her father until he died and looked after her granddaughter for the two years prior to her moving, she relished the opportunity to enjoy herself and loved the social opportunities available in the Costa Blanca. Her use of 'I just think' again reflects that home for her in Spain is chosen and pragmatic, since her emotional connection to England; illustrated by 'I don't feel England's my home any more' has been fractured:

'Well, I've upped and moved and I just think this is my home now. I don't feel England's my home anymore.' (Margot)

Myra was also determined to make a successful life in Spain and this is reflected by the way she talks about the UK and Spain. Like Olive, Myra also escaped from difficult circumstances, her ageing mother needed care and her family thought that she should fulfil this role once she retired. Myra resisted her family's expectations and instead moved to Spain. She rejected the UK in the present, resenting the presence of 'illegal immigrants' there and was happy to be surrounded by her compatriots in Spain. Myra like Margot presents Spain as home because that is where she has chosen to live, but she enjoys holidays in the UK as that is where her daughter and granddaughter are:

'I live here, this is my home but I go back to England for holidays and see my daughter and granddaughter. I've got no intention of going back though.' (Myra)

Cynthia had lived in Spain for longer than the other women, and was the only one who could speak Spanish, and she has also been involved in marketing properties to British people. She and her husband took early retirement to move to Spain, partly for the benefit of her husband's health and also due to feeling pushed out of the UK, through the presence of 'others' in the area where she had lived. She successfully overcame a number of obstacles in Spain, for example 'mixing with the Spanish when she can' and managed to construct a positive grandmother identity while away from her grandchildren. Throughout her narrative she cast herself as having agency, as being knowledgeable about Spain, highlighting some of the 'problems' involved when people move from the UK:

'One of the biggest problems is that one of the parties doesn't really want to be here and I found that when I was selling houses and funnily enough it was the man that wanted to come and live here and the lady who didn't.' (Cynthia)

Cynthia was placed at the centre of a social scene, being one of the two co-founders of the Silver Ladies club, which also gave her the opportunity to socialise away from her husband. She is emphatic about staying in Spain and says in four different ways that she enjoys the quality of life there and presents Spain as the place where she has chosen to be:

> 'I'm happy to be here and I'm staying here. I think the biggest thing is that it's a very relaxed (1), easy going (2), chilled out (3), stress-free (4) life.' (Cynthia)

In the following narrative excerpt, when Cynthia says 'that's about it' she is highlighting that the familiar retail opportunities in the UK are the only thing she misses; in all other aspects Spain wins every time. This is in keeping with her positive story about Spain:

> 'The only thing I will say is that I miss the shops. Yeah, that's about it.' (Cynthia)

Previously, Mabel described herself as 'a political animal' and as 'hating age prejudice' in the UK leading to feelings of dislocation. She welcomed the opportunity to exercise 'freedom' in Spain after discharging her surrogate parenting duties towards her grandson. She 'loved Spain' and although came from a more privileged background to the other women, she did not position herself as being superior or particularly different; instead, she welcomed the opportunity to socialise with other women. Being older than the other participants at 83, Mabel retired in her 'fourth age' and had even planned ahead for her burial in Spain, having no intention of ever going back to the UK. Here she positions herself as an older person conscious of reaching the latter stage of her life, and Spain is the place where she plans to stay:

> 'I've even arranged my funeral. I shall be buried on a shelf...I pass it on the motorway; on the N332 and I think that's going to be my future home, all done and paid for.' (Mabel)

Ambivalent feelings about Spain as home

> 'I think that what anybody contemplating living here needs to know is that it's not paradise. It's not going to be the answer to all your problems.' (Joy)

Ambivalence often precipitates the decision to migrate, and can also be a product of migration (Benson, 2011a) as both Olive and Joy's experiences illustrate. The circumstances surrounding Olive's moving to Spain could be significant. As noted in Chapter Four, she reluctantly took early retirement following a back injury and this also coincided with her divorce: she wanted to escape a difficult set of circumstances in the UK and Spain was an option. Although Olive had made several friends, she sometimes found social contact intrusive and also experienced difficulties establishing herself in Spain. Visiting her family in the UK or in her country of origin heightened her feelings of insecurity:

> 'Every time I go to England or [country of birth] and then [come back] to Spain I feel that I have to start all over again, kind of lonely and disorientated and disrupted.' (Olive)

Olive was certain that she would not move back to the UK although her children and grandchildren live there. However, she is also unsure about staying in Spain, since the prospect of being by herself there and living alone as she aged was not attractive. For Olive, 'home' is her country of birth, and the place to which she eventually planned to return:

> 'I'd like to but even though I would like to, I can't see myself [staying in Spain] forever because being on my own first, secondly, is when you get old living on your own is not very good for anybody. What I've been thinking is that maybe later I'll go back home to my sister living together with my sister, my family, eventually back home to [country of origin].' (Olive)

Retirement migration is not always the last stage on someone's migration trajectory and it is common for return migration to take place in the fourth age (King et al, 1998). Originally from south-east Asia, Olive had previously had a mobile life; first living in Germany as a young woman and then in the UK for 30 years prior to moving to Spain. Here, she also presents her country of origin as a potential escape route (Elliott and Urry, 2010, cited in Torkington, 2012).

Joy was keen to leave the UK as she described it as 'a totally crap place to be', yet she also had very ambivalent feelings about being in Spain. Throughout her narrative she positioned herself as a 'good' wife and mother, moving to Spain for the benefit of her husband and returning to the UK every three months to see her sons. Joy's ambivalence could in part relate to her husband's ill health and the uncertainty surrounding this, but she also expressed disdain about her compatriots, did not want to socialise with them or join the Silver Ladies club:

> 'Now, we just went back in April because my husband was diagnosed here in Spain as having liver cancer and because he had private health insurance in UK we went back to UK for the operation, but other things intervened…So we've only been back in Spain for two weeks now and I'm afraid that I have become slightly disenchanted, although I expect I was disenchanted before.' (Joy)

Joy's attachment to the UK was due to her sons being there and Spain's proximity was a bonus. However, she did not feel 'at home' in either place which compounded her feelings of insecurity and displacement.

The UK as home

Vera, Deidre, Jenny and Agnes – those women who wanted to return to the UK – describe it as home and Vera and Jenny in particular express a strong attachment. Vera quickly became disillusioned with life in Spain: her negative experience of being on the committee of the urbanisation and perceptions of corruption and bureaucracy impaired her enjoyment of life there. Both she and Deidre had originally planned to stay in Spain for ten years or so, but this experience combined with her intolerance of the weather, feelings of antipathy towards her compatriots, coupled with rising house prices in the UK, precipitated an earlier return. Although she wishes to return to the UK; Spain is her home for the moment because that is where she has chosen to live, but she is very clear that the UK is the place where her 'heart is': where she feels 'at home'. Vera's narrative illuminates that that belonging to places can be complex and multi-layered, in this way it was possible to be of one place temporarily, yet ultimately and always from another. Here she positions herself as liking the idea of Spain (the exotic) but presents the UK as home:

> 'I mean, people on the plane will say "Are you going on holiday?" and I say, "No I'm going home," and I say that in the sense that's where my house is, not where my heart is, where my house is. England yes, it's never changed. I can never think of anywhere but England as home.' (Vera)

In Vera's narrative there is transformation of subjectivities (Day Sclater, 1998a). Earlier she exoticised Spain, describing living there as 'exciting' and 'thrilling', yet for her the UK remains home. She also talked about the revival of community spirit in Spain, but the superficial nature of social networks for her did not compensate for long-standing friends and family relationships, in particular her daughter.

As at the start of the quest, part of the process of return involves imagining a future life in the new destination, in this case the UK. Vera focuses on the cultural activities which she misses while in Spain:

> 'I'd be able to utilise libraries in England which would be
> a very nice thing to do. I'd be able to visit the cinema and
> the theatre.' (Vera)

Like Vera, Deidre wanted to return 'home' to the UK. Deidre had not settled in Spain and was looking forward to going back to the UK:

> 'We'll move back to [Yorkshire] and move into [Vera's
> daughter's] flat. I'm perfectly happy to do that.' (Deidre)

Deidre's pre-migration imaginings of the good life in Spain did not quite materialise, she struggled with the heat and did not feel affinity with her compatriots. Instead she preferred the company of people in the UK she felt 'deep for'. Deidre, too, imagines how their lives would be once they returned 'home':

> 'I think one huge thing for both of us, we're going to be
> able to play golf because we can't afford to play in Spain…
> but in England you get the municipal courses so we can
> play golf once a week and that's going to be for us a huge
> thing 'cos we both love it.' (Deidre)

Women who emphasise what they miss about the UK are those who express a wish to return; while unsurprisingly those who wish to stay in Spain minimise this and focus on the positives of being in Spain.

Agnes moved to Spain for the benefit of her husband's health. She previously presented herself as compliant in the decision to move to Spain and as a 'good wife', but in spite of making friends had never felt 'at home'. Agnes did not like living on an urbanisation and for her being in Spain represented constraint rather than freedom and she was relieved to be returning to the familiarity of the UK. Again, she presents the decision to return to the UK as her husband's, illuminating household decision-making processes, although this time she is happy with the decision, illustrated through her use of "thank goodness":

> 'No, no we've decided, well my husband's decided, at last, thank goodness, that he wants to go back.' (Agnes)

Jenny only agreed to migrate to Spain with her husband as she thought her daughter and family would also be moving there. However, this had not happened and it was now unlikely that they would. Jenny did not enjoy being in Spain, she was frustrated by her husband's lack of interest in seeing other parts of the country and felt restricted and trapped living on the urbanisation. For Jenny, being away from 'home' appeared to be very painful and she says here four times in this short extract of her narrative that she wants to be in England. She does not want to live in Spain until 'the end' of her life. Her final comment relates to how she felt when she returned to the UK for a holiday:

> 'I would like to go back to England at the end (1)...I think after so many years I'd still like to go back to England (2). I don't think I want to spend the rest of my life in Spain (3)...I do miss England (4)...It's lovely. It really is lovely. The first time I went back I had tears in my eyes.' (Jenny)

However, Jenny is trapped because her husband refuses to return to the UK. She talks about the 'battle' she is faced with to get him to change his mind; yet this is hopeless since he has no intentions of returning:

> '[Husband] doesn't want to go back so I have a battle on my hands. If [daughter and granddaughter] come out to live eventually I will stay in Spain to have them closer to me; but if they don't, I've got to keep on at [husband] to say that I want to go back and see how it goes. But he doesn't [want to]; he's got no intentions of going back to England.' (Jenny)

Living betwixt and between

For those women who live in Spain for part of the year, irrespective of whether they are happy with the arrangement or not, the UK is presented as home. Bernice talks about the UK as 'home' and Spain as 'away', and this appears to be straightforward for her:

'We've been home quite a bit because, for different occasions, you know, but we, I can't tell you exactly how much time we've been here, three months and other times about six weeks, or something like that.' (Bernice)

Throughout her narrative Bernice emphasises the benefits of having 'the best of both worlds'. However, in the following extract she suggests that she would be willing to move to Spain permanently, but this would involve selling their house in the UK. At first she indicates that she did not want to sell the house 'at home' but then casts her husband as having the final say, again illuminating dynamics within her household:

'If we stayed permanently we'd want to move again and it'd mean selling at home and I don't want to sell, well he [husband] doesn't want to sell at home.' (Bernice)

Viv, like Bernice, enjoys living in Spain part time. For her the UK represents home and she would not contemplate moving to Spain permanently:

'At home we've been there 30 years, so when you've been there that long you don't move.' (Viv)

Similarly, for Enid, Northern Ireland is home:

'Northern Ireland will always be my home.' (Enid)

Enid is disillusioned with life in the Costa Blanca. She is disappointed in the area she lived in, does not like living on an urbanisation nor does she feel a sense of belonging to the available social networks.

Locating home and community

Algia – longing is what [they] share but nostos – the return home is what divides [them]. (Boym, 2001, xvi)

Although integration is more difficult for retired people (King et al, 2000; Huber and O'Reilly, 2004), when considering how the women construct belonging to 'home', the concept identificational integration (King and Skeldon, 2010) is useful. Identificational integration denotes feelings of belonging and can be understood as being influenced by – but not contingent upon – structural, cultural and interactive integration. Structural integration involves citizenship and associated rights: the women featured were free to migrate to Spain due to fluid borders in the European Union and their British citizenship. Cultural integration involves conforming to host society norms, yet these women imported British (or English) cultural practices to Spain and there was no expectation from the Spanish government that they would integrate into Spanish society. Interactive integration relates to social networks: these women were unable to bridge to their Spanish hosts and formed networks with compatriots with similar backgrounds.

To different degrees and in multiple ways, all of the women featured shared a disillusionment with the UK in the present and an idealisation of its past. However, once in Spain, they found that they were effectively living in bounded settlements, almost exclusively with people from their own ethnic group, which represents a structural boundary. O'Reilly (2007b) refers to a 'mobility enclosure dialectic' which denotes the apparent contradictions in British migrants' status and experience once in Spain. Although boundary spanning is facilitated by upper and more proximate structural layers, their equivocal position in Spain is shaped by their British citizenship and Britain's position in the European Union (O'Reilly, 2007b). For these women, living in diaspora space (Brah, 1996), location shapes and reinforces group and individual identity. Women also reconstitute boundaries through their agency, forming networks predicated on their class, age, ethnic and gender positionalities. Simultaneously, women's positionalities are effectively reinforced by their dislocation from their hosts, their inability to speak Spanish, their diasporic status and their social networks and practices (Temple, 1999; Anthias, 2002).

For those women who wish to remain in Spain, superficial social networks with quest companions suffice. Those who wish to return to the UK on the other hand, construct the UK as a place to where they wanted to return, and where social networks are longer standing and more meaningful. Women see themselves as English, rather than British, and this represents an 'old' form of 'patriotism', existing away from the UK. I previously described women in Spain as patriots of the past; they can also be understood to be nostalgic patriots since their movement across space also represents a movement back in time and a rejection of modern Britain.

Women who move to Spain construct complex and shifting belonging to both the UK and Spain as places. The role of the imagination and in particular the use of nostalgia in constructing an idyll is important, across space, or where one is 'placed'. Further, the issue of home is also multi-faceted; it generally denotes the place where the women feel an overriding sense of belonging. Also, significantly, home is constructed as the place where people want to be and it is possible to feel that more than one place is home; however, this does not have to be consistent or mean the same thing for everybody.

The concepts 'transnationalism' and 'transmigrant' are useful to understand belonging to multiple places and the interlocking relationship between networks and positionalities. 'Transnationalism' can be understood as the ways that people construct simultaneous relationships to two places (Gustafson, 2008; Levitt, 2012; van Noorloos, 2013), while 'transmigrant', denotes migrants whose lives and identities bridge international borders (Glick-Schiller et al, 1995). The notions of transnationalism and transmigrant highlight the overlapping relationship between different forms of belonging regarding degrees of mobility and cross-border practices and individual and collective belonging to both sending and host countries, social networks, and cultural expression in the new country (Gustafson, 2008). To a degree the women featured can be described as 'transmigrants' (Cronin, 2006; O'Reilly, 2000a; 2003; 2007a) since they were from one place and of another. They reconstruct their English ethnic identity in Spain, in part through networks with other migrants from the UK and this is also influenced by their positionalites. However, there are limits to the application of transmigrant as a category to describe these women (also see O'Reilly, 2007a). They do not embody 'placeless capital' (Papastergiadis, 2000, cited in O'Reilly, 2007a): instead, their capital is shaped by their social and spatial locations and they are on the margins in Spain. On several levels therefore, place remains important and women's positionalities affects the ways (or not) that they are 'transnational'. Here Vertovec's (2010) premise regarding theorising transnationalism is useful: 'Rather than a single theory of transnationalism and migration, we may do better to theorise a typology of transnationalisms and the conditions that affect them' (Vertovec, 2010, 576).

Conclusion

Like community, 'home' embodies notions of belonging encompassing ←
places and people and can have multiple, simultaneous meanings. For example, it is possible to be of one place and from another and refer to both places as home while feeling belonging to one or both in varying degrees and in different ways (Cronin, 2006). In this way, home is pragmatic and contingent on experiences and intention and the ending embedded in both plot typologies is the place to where women construct belonging, or home and community. Being 'at

home', then, involves place, time, emotions and being with others like us, representing belonging and community and is also shaped by positionalities. Moreover, women's constructions of 'home' can be understood as representing a barometer of their quality of life or intimacy with the world (Anthias, 2006).

Women who moved to Spain construct complex and shifting belonging to both the UK and Spain as places. The role of the imagination and in particular the use of nostalgia in constructing an idyll is important, across space, or where one was 'placed'. Further, the issue of home is also multi-faceted; it generally denoted the place where the women felt an overriding sense of belonging. Also, significantly, home is constructed as the place where people wanted to be and it is possible to feel that more than one place was home; however this does not have to be consistent or mean the same thing for everybody. In other words, 'Longing might be what we share as human beings, but that doesn't prevent us from telling very different stories of belonging and non-belonging' (Boym, 2001, 41).

In the concluding chapter a final analysis of the relationship between nostalgia, belonging and community in retirement migration as illuminated through an interpretive narrative approach is presented.

CONCLUSION

Nostalgia, belonging and community: linking time and space

Introduction

I premised at the outset that the idea of community is often romantic and utopian, idealising and evoking a bygone age. Often considered to have been 'lost' through modernity, community has also been hailed as the solution to social 'problems' by successive governments in the UK. From the New Right to the present Conservative-led coalition government, community has become synonymous with a relinquishment of responsibility by the state (Hoggett et al, 1997). When the women made their move to Spain, community in policy circles was presented by the then government, as a panacea to the lack of social cohesion among diverse ethnic groups. Exploring how 'community' is presented and constructed in new contexts and examining how and to what women constructed belonging, illuminates their agency and positionalities within wider structural contexts and also processes of social change and continuity.

The women featured orchestrated their own solution to non-belonging in the UK: they chose to leave the UK but found themselves once more on the margins in Spain. As a result, they needed to forge and construct new forms of belonging and community and review and revisit old ones. These women constructed belonging and community, based on being of and from a place, through social networks and this was also shaped by their social locations. Although community could at times be superficial and tenuous, for them, its presence denoted a better quality of life. Isolated diasporic communities like this one – formed through migration – often look back to the past to create a sense of belonging among members (O'Reilly, 2000a; 2002). Nostalgic constructions of belonging and community are key to how these women gave meaning to their lives through an orientation to the past. In the final analysis I revisit the abiding importance of unravelling belonging to different representations of community to understand retired British women's experiences of migration to Spain.

Place, networks and positionalities

In the current context of global movement, place is still important since people still construct belonging to places (Cronin, 2006), social interaction is located 'somewhere' (Jackson, 1999 and Stevenson, 1999, cited in Sherlock, 2002) and 'people and place interact' (MacLennan, 2000). Place then, can be understood as an enduring representation of community, and provides the context for women's networks to be formed, and also shapes and reinforces their positionalities. Networks – or belonging to groups – are also linked to place and social location. Belonging to networks is complex and fluid through migration and the creation of new communities out of one's original context, reflecting the rapidity of social change and movement. Where someone originates from influences the kind of networks in which they engage and the role of common language and shared background are also significant. Instead of presenting women as inhabiting social categories and these 'intersecting', I have focused on the processes involved in positionalities translocating, through examining their narratives. These women have multiple locations, positions and belongings and translocation involves movement across positions (Anthias, 2008) and space and time. In this way, women's gendered, class and ethnic positionalities are all significant in shaping belonging and community construction in migration. Their positionalities are shaped by context and structure, influence agency and also mediate between them.

To put simply, women's social positions and experiences are gendered, classed and shaped by ethnicity and age: their gendered experiences are classed; class experiences gendered, and their age and ethnic identification and ascription also shape these and each other. These delineations are not fixed, and they forge, reinforce, construct and structure how and to what they belong. What is also important is that these groups do not constitute homogeneous categories and the boundaries between and within them are socially constructed (Anthias et al, 2012). The idea of translocation is useful as it captures the malleability, fluidity and agglomeration of social locations or positions that people inhabit and construct, and it also weaves in temporal and spatial dimensions: 'to think of *trans*locations opens up not only thinking of relocations but also of the multiplicity of locations involved in time and space, and in terms of connections between the past, the present and the future' (Anthias, 2008, 15). Moving from the idea of 'dislocation' which assumes a fixed location, translocation is helpful in understanding the multiple and shifting landscapes which frame social locations. These landscapes can be social, material, imagined and are constructed. In this way, to be 'dislocated' at one level, for example, through being away from one's original context through retirement migration does not mean that dislocation occurs in other areas (Anthias, 2008).

Belonging, community and narrative

Of course narrative analysis is not the only way of gaining insight into people's lived experiences: people focus on the nadirs and zeniths of their lives when they narrate (Anthias, 2002), and narratives are fragile (Giddens, 1991) and only one of many possible stories we can tell about ourselves. However, I have not presented narratives as some kind of special representation of reality (Atkinson, 1997), or as an 'empathetic appreciation of personal accounts' (Atkinson, 2009, 4), rather as subjective and an interpretation. Using a thematic and structural narrative approach to explore belonging and community in migration enables links to be made between the micro, or lives lived and social change particularly within the macro context of migration in retirement. Women who moved from the UK to Spain examined their lives through recounting narratives (Ricoeur, 1984) which enabled me to meaningfully relate these private and public realms (Mills, 1959), and to evaluate the links between women's unique biographies, their social locations and within the context of wider social structures (Riessman, 2000a; Temple, 2001; Benson, 2012). The idea of belonging is central to our understanding of how people give meaning to their lives, or their constructions of intimacy with the world (Anthias, 2006) and a structural narrative approach allows us to go beyond *what* is said. Intimacy with the world is achieved through constructing belonging to different forms of community, and nostalgia reflects and constructs intimacy with the world through narrative by chronotopically linking time and space. It is also possible to perceive narrative as a means of making other linkages in relation to 'the how' (processes) and 'the who' (positionalites) in constructions of belonging and community within wider structural contexts.

Increased choice and rapid social change can lead to uncertainty rather than freedom (Skey, 2011) and the need for 'ontological security' (Giddens, 1991) – represented here by belonging and community – increases in times of rapid social change. After people's physiological and safety needs are met, the third level of human needs which need to be satisfied involves feelings of belonging (Maslow, 1943); and belonging, or the processes of feeling or being a part of rather than apart from, involves the translocation of physical, temporal and social locations and the work of the imagination. Narratives can be understood to simultaneously both represent and construct community, and how people prefigure belonging through narrative illuminates how they see themselves in relation to place, networks and social location/positionalities and wider social structures.

Nostalgia and community revisited

> At first glance, nostalgia is a longing for a place, but actually it is a yearning for a different time. (Boym, 2001, xv)

As I have suggested nostalgia is an elusive concept and is often represented as an emotion or feeling (Boym, 2001) which can be examined at will (Dickinson and Erben, 2006) and this is reflected and constructed through narrative. I suggested that nostalgia could be seen both within the context of, and as an outcome of rapid social change, since 'Nostalgic manifestations are side effects of the teleology of progress' (Boym, 2001, 10). Nostalgic recollections occur in linear time (Boym, 2001; Dickinson and Erben, 2006); however, nostalgic recollections are not actual memories, rather they are attempts to recreate a lost past. For the women in Spain, belonging and community are constructed through a sense of nostalgic intimacy with the world. If intimacy is compromised then nostalgia constructs and reflects belonging; in other words, nostalgia bridges this gap. Nostalgia encompasses space, time, emotions and lifestyle (Chaitin, Linstroth and Hiller, 2009) and time and space are linked through nostalgia as are the past and the present.

The concept of nostalgia therefore is invaluable in understanding belonging and community, in the context of retirement migration; and, as I have already suggested, it can be understood as both an idealisation of the past and as bringing the past into the present (Dickinson and Erben, 2006). The nostalgic meta-narrative of the UK governments construct community as a vehicle to cure society. The counter-narratives of many of the women who moved to Spain also implicitly use nostalgia to explain their actions in leaving the UK. Nostalgia relates to an imagined, idealised past not actually remembered or experienced by the women featured, or by policy makers in the UK. However, the use of nostalgia in constructing this ideal is important since both meta- and counter-narratives can be understood as conveying the work of the imagination.

It is useful here to identify two distinct but related kinds of nostalgia: restorative and reflective (Boym, 2001). Restorative nostalgia 'stresses *nostos* and attempts a transhistorical reconstruction of the lost home' (Boym, 2001, xviii). Reflective nostalgia, on the other hand, 'thrives in *algia,* the longing itself' (Boym, 2001, xviii). Like belonging and community, reflective and restorative nostalgia are both symbolic and utilitarian. Belonging and community can be understood as being ephemeral and intangible in terms of reflective nostalgia, and as pragmatic and tangible as restorative nostalgia. Salazar (2014) emphasises the significance of socio-cultural imaginaries in lifestyle migration, which are utopian and spatially and temporally distant, and O'Reilly (2014) suggests that imaginings are often nostalgic. Reflective and restorative nostalgia reflect the 'social imaginary' (O'Reilly, 2014), and involves both agency and structure. Restorative nostalgia, too, reflects agency within the context of social structures, and reproduces social, spatial and temporal locations.

Heimweh, or homesickness is the pain felt by someone 'away' from 'home' or what is familiar. Home can therefore be a place, a time or both and nostalgia links these in narrative. Nostos, the return home can be understood as a return to another time and can also be achieved in a different place. In this way the return home denotes going back in time as well as travelling across space. Algia is the longing, the pain, for another past (time) as well as a lost place. This was particularly important for the women featured since they were on the margins, and felt dislocation in both the UK and Spain. Nostalgia provides familiarity and safety in an unfamiliar social world which is changing rapidly. It represents an antidote to modernity and social change. We cannot halt modernity but we can preserve or halt our position and relationship to the social world through nostalgia. The past is idealised and brought into the present through narrative which both reflects and constructs it. Nostalgia therefore represents a significant part of how belonging and community are constructed and presented. However, in spite of nostalgia's centrality to my analysis, like community, it ultimately remains an elusive, ephemeral and contested concept since:

> Nostalgia is akin to unrequited love, only we are not sure about the identity of our lost beloved. (Boym, 2001, 274)

Afterword

Vera and Deirdre moved back to Yorkshire in 2005, and Agnes and her husband moved back to Norfolk in the same year. Enid and her husband sold their holiday home in the Costa Blanca in 2006, and bought one in Florida. In 2006 Jenny left her husband and returned to the UK and rented a property close to where her daughter lived. Lillian and her husband bought a house further inland in southern Spain and kept the house in the Costa Blanca as a holiday home.

Throughout this book I have emphasised that knowledge is contextually and temporally specific and it's important to emphasise again that women's retirement migration was also contextually contingent. Since the fieldwork took place, the structural contexts enabling retirement migration have shifted: the economic crisis in 2008 has affected housebuilding and house prices in the Alicante province (De La Paz and White, 2012) and there has also been a reduction in British migration to Spain and an increase in return migration (Huete et al, 2013). It is unclear what the impact on retirement migration will be in the future, but issues to consider include longer retirement and geo-environmental concerns.

Notes

Preface
[1] Which for the purposes of this book I will refer to as 'The Silver Ladies'.

One: Retiring to the Costas: British women's narratives of nostalgia, belonging and community

[1] The Costa Blanca is the commercial name for the coastal region in the province of Alicante in South East Spain.

[2] 'A Place in the Sun' is the name of a UK Channel Four TV programme about buying properties abroad.

[3] EU migrants are not legally entitled to stay in Spain more than 90 days without returning to the UK or home country or applying for a Temporary Residence Permit. If people stay for over six months a full residential permit – *Tarjeta de Residencia*, initially for two years, then in five-year periods – must be applied for. At the time when the fieldwork took place, Spanish authorities did not enforce this, hence why so many of the research participants did not apply for residencia. However, since July 2012, a royal decree was issued making this mandatory, and placed further requirements on EU migrants to demonstrate that they could financially support themselves in Spain. Regarding healthcare, the Spanish system is contribution-based, rather than residence-based like the NHS in the UK. UK state pensioners and early retirees can register and access Spanish healthcare but they need to deregister with their GP in the UK. If people return to the UK then they need to deregister with the Spanish authorities and re-register in the UK.

[4] Examples of other residential typologies of migrants used by researchers in the field include O'Reilly's (2000a) full and returning residents who no longer had a residence in the UK (seasonal visitors; peripatetic visitors who often owned properties in Spain but still worked in the UK; and tourists or holiday makers); and Huete and Mantecon's (2012) categorisation of migrants to the Costa Blanca (permanent residents (owner-occupiers and registered); temporary (renting) and registered; second home owners (unregistered); and tourists).

[5] Chronotope refers to a literary device connecting time and space and this is discussed in detail in the following chapter.

Two: Conceptualising, theorising and narrating retirement migration

[1] See King, 2012b for a detailed historical overview of migration theory.

[2] Salazar (2014) refers to this as 'failed' migration and highlights the lack of research on this issue.

[3] Note, though, that Bakewell uses a critical realist epistemology to critique structuration.

[4] I use positionalities rather than habitus as the meso level of interaction between structure and agency.

[5] Some writers use discourse in a similar way to how I use narrative, see for example, Lundstrom, 2014.

[6] Vieda Skultans (1998) examines the narratives of Latvian 'forest brothers', denoting men and women who took refuge in forests during the post-war decade.

[7] This is sometimes included with the general term 'structure' of a narrative rather than separate from structure.

[8] Oliver, 2008; Benson, 2012; Korpela and Dervin, 2013 use a thematic narrative analysis to make sense of migration experiences.

[9] I discuss my positionalities in the following chapter.

[10] Deconstruction describes an approach to textual analysis whereby the text is dismantled into components through multiple interpretations.

Three: Locating the women: macro, meso and micro contexts

[1] The concept of agency is linked to power and influence, relating to the ability to exercise choice (Giddens, 1986).

[2] The euro replaced the peseta in 2002.

[3] This is based on my own experience during the fieldwork.

[4] However, it is worth noting that inequalities among older people are often overlooked since ageing is sanitised and homogenised in popular culture (Conway, 2003).

[5] O'Reilly (2012) uses Bourdieu's concept habitus to denote the mediating layer between structure and agency in migration.

[6] It is important to note that I do not see positionalities as disembodied but instead inscribed with social values, similar to how Giddens (1986) uses social identity.

[7] The third age (Laslett, 1989, cited in Oliver, 2008 denotes 'young old' aged 60–74 years while the fourth age, or 'old old' begins at 75 years.

[8] Vera and I met at university in 1991.

[9] Abdikarim Ismail Ahmed, known as Abdi, from the Habr Yunis clan in Burao, Northern Somalia. Abdi rejects a clan identity, only identifying as 'Somali'.

[10] Margaret Eunice Andrews, known as Eunice, from Crawford village in Lancashire. I include my parents' names and these details as I think this effectively invokes their positionalities, and also highlights how my own have been shaped.

[11] Apart from a brief period when he was employed as a ballroom dancing instructor and another when he ran a cafe in Sheffield.

[12] Chosen by my mother.

[13] Apart from Olive.

Four: Boundary spanning and reconstitution: retirement migration and the search for community

[1] The term 'nostalgia' was introduced in 1688 by Johannes Hofer (1669–1752).

[2] Although Bauman (2001) argues that the security that community brings results in a loss of freedom.

[3] My structural narrative approach to generating knowledge is discussed in detail in the following chapter.

[4] Huber and O'Reilly (2004) suggest instead using the term 'heimat' as an alternative to community. This is discussed in Chapter Nine.

[5] Modernity refers to capitalist, urban, and post-capitalist society.

Five: Leaving the UK: motives, agency and decision-making processes

[1] Influenced by Taylor (1969) and Beshers (1967).

[2] Often used as the opening line in a story to signify that a series of events will follow.

[3] Originally articulated by Radcliffe (1991, cited in Hoang, 2011) and Chant and Radcliffe (1992).

[4] Émile Durkheim termed this 'anomie'.

Six: Living in Spain: 'idyllisation' and realisation

[1] The women's Mediterranean idyll embodies elements of Benson and O'Reilly's (2009) depiction of the rural idyll, but fall more accurately under the definition of residential tourism as a form of lifestyle migration.

[2] Further obstacles, such as quest companions/other British people/social networks/ not being able to speak Spanish/no contact with Spanish people/how to be a good yet remote grandmother, are discussed in the following chapters.

[3] For example HP sauce, marmite, 'English' bread, Heinz beans etc.

[4] See Benson 2011a for a discussion of authenticity in relation to middle-class Britons living in the Lot in France.

[5] Falaraki is another popular British tourist destination on the Greek island of Rhodes.

Seven: Belonging to networks: reconciling agency and positionalities

[1] The 'Shamrock Club' and 'Jilly's' are pseudonyms.

[2] The remainder took place in the women's homes.

[3] Apart from one Norwegian woman who spoke English fluently.

[4] Cynthia was the only woman who could speak Spanish sufficiently to 'get by'.

[5] O'Reilly, 2000b and Skey, 2011 refer to Britishness as 'us'.

[6] See Ahmed, 2012, for a discussion of how belonging to social networks can also be predicated on acceptable behaviour, in the case of Celia's account of her neighbour, an alcoholic.

Eight: Renegotiating family relationships: managing intimacy from a distance

[1] See also O'Reilly, 2000b, where she frames women in the Costa del Sol as exchanging their relationships with grandchildren for the freedom of migration.

[2] Enid and Viv living in Spain part time did not feel that their relationships with their children (none had grandchildren) were altered by their being in Spain. Agnes did not want to talk about her relationship with her children as she was estranged from her two daughters.

[3] The fieldwork took place before Skype, and mobile telephone use was expensive. The women kept in touch with family in the UK by landline telephone.

Nine: Locating 'home' and community: the end point of plot movement

[1] There is no translation of *heimat* into English.

[2] I borrow this from Sigur Ros' film about their homecoming in Iceland.

[3] Apart from in relation to learning Spanish.

References

Ackers, L, 2000, *Shifting spaces: Women, citizenship and migration within the European Union*, Bristol: Policy Press

Adams, M, 2007, *Self and social change*, London: Sage

Ahmed, A, 2010, *Home and away: British women's narratives of community in Spain*, PhD thesis, University of Central Lancashire

Ahmed, A, 2011, Belonging out of context: The intersection of place, networks and ethnic identity among retired British migrants living in the Costa Blanca, *Journal of Identity and Migration Studies* 5, 2, 2–19

Ahmed, A, 2012, Networks among retired British women in the Costa Blanca: Insiders, outsiders, 'club capital' and 'limited liability', *Urbanities* 2, 2, 95–112

Ahmed, A, 2013, Structural narrative analysis: Understanding experiences of lifestyle migration through two plot typologies, *Qualitative Inquiry* 19, 3, 232–43

Ahmed, S, Fortier, A-M, 2003, Re-imagining communities, *International Journal of Cultural Studies* 6, 3, 251–9

Alexander, C, Edwards, R, Temple, B, 2007, Contesting cultural communities: language, ethnicity and citizenship in Britain, *Journal of Ethnic and Migration Studies* 33, 5, 783–800

Alibhai-Brown, Y, 2007, *No place like home*, London: Virago

Amit, V, 2012, Community and disjuncture: The creativity and uncertainty of everyday engagement, in V Amit, N Rapport (eds) *Community, cosmopolitanism and the problem of human commonality*, pp 3–73, London: Pluto Press

Amit, V, Rapport, N, 2002, *The trouble with community: Anthropological reflections on movement, identity and collectivity*, London: Pluto Press

Anderson, B, 1983, *Imagined communities*, London: Verso

Anderson, B, 2006, *Imagined communities: Reflections on the origin and spread of nationalism*, London, New York: Verso

Anderson, ML, Hill Collins, P (eds), 1992, *Race, class and gender: An anthology*, Belmont, CA: Wadsworth/Thomson Learning

Andrews, M, 2004, Memories of mother: Counter-narratives of early maternal influence, in M Andrews, M Bamberg (eds) *Considering counter-narratives: Narration and resistance*, Amsterdam: John Benjamins Publishing Company

Andrews, M, Bamberg, M (eds), 2004, *Considering counter-narratives: Narration and resistance*, Amsterdam: John Benjamins Publishing Company

Anthias, F, 1998a, Evaluating diaspora: Beyond ethnicity?, *Sociology* 32, 3, 557–80

Anthias, F, 1998b, Rethinking social divisions: Some notes towards a theoretical framework, *Sociological Review* 46, 3, 506–35

Anthias, F, 2002, Where do I belong? Narrating identity and translocational positionality, *Ethnicities* 2, 4, 491–515

Anthias, F, 2006, Belonging in a globalising and unequal world: Rethinking translocations, in N Yuval-Davis, K Kannabiran, U Vieten, 2006, *The situated politics of belonging*, London: Sage Publications

Anthias, F, 2008, Thinking through the lens of translocational positionality: An intersectionality frame for understanding identity and belonging, *Translocations: Migration and social change* 4, 1, 5–20

Anthias, F, Cederberg, M, 2009, Narratives of ethnicity, resources and social capital, *Journal of Ethnic and Migration Studies* 35, 6, 901–17

Anthias, F, Kontos, M, Morokvasic, M (eds), 2012, *Paradoxes of integration: Female migrants in Europe*, New York: Springer

Arber, S, Timonen, V, 2012, Grandparenting in the 21st century: New directions, in S Arber, V Timonen (eds) *Contemporary grandparenting: Changing family relationships in global contexts,* Bristol: Policy Press

Armstrong, MJ, 2005, Grandchildren's influence on grandparents, *Journal of Intergenerational Relationships* 3, 2, 7–21

Atkinson, P, 1997, Narrative turn or blind alley?, *Qualitative Health Research* 7, 3, 325–44

Atkinson, P, 2009, Illness narratives revisited: The failure of narrative reductionism, *Sociological Research Online* 14, 5, www.socresonline.org.uk

Back, L, Keith, M, Khan, A, Shukra, K, Solomos, J, 2002, The return of assimilationism: Race, multiculturalism and New Labour, *Sociological Research Online* 7, 2, www.socresonline.org.uk

Bakewell, O, 2010, Some reflections on structure and agency in migration theory, *Journal of Ethnic and Migration Studies* 36, 10, 1689–708

Bakhtin, MM, 1981, *The dialogic imagination: Four essays*, R Holquist (ed), sixteenth paperback printing, Austin, TX: University of Texas Press, 2006

Ballard, JG, 1997, *Cocaine nights*, London: Flamingo

Bamberg, M, 2004, Considering counter narratives, in M Bamberg, M Andrews (eds) *Considering counter narratives: Narrating, resisting, making sense*, pp 351–71, Amsterdam: John Benjamins

Banks, SP, 2009, International ties across borders: Grandparenting narratives by expatriate retirees in Mexico, *Journal of Aging Studies* 23, 178–87

Bates, JS, 2009, Generative grandfathering: a conceptual framework for nurturing grandchildren, *Marriage and Family Review*, 45, 4, 331–52

Bauman, Z, 2001, *Community: Seeking safety in an insecure world*, Cambridge: Polity Press

Beck, U, 1992, *Risk society*, London: Sage

Beider, H, 2012, *Race, housing and community: Perspectives on policy and practice*, Malaysia: Wiley-Blackwell

Bell, J, Clisby, S, Craig, G, Measor, L, Petrie, S, Stanley, N, 2004, *Living on the edge: Sexual behaviour and young parenthood in seaside and rural areas*, London: Department of Health

Bendassolli, PF, 2013, Theory building in qualitative research: Reconsidering the problem of Induction, *Forum: Qualitative Social Research* 14, 1, www.qualitative-research.net

Bengston, VL, 1975, Generations and family effects in value socialization, *American Sociological Review* 40, 34, 358–71

Bengston, VL, 2001, Beyond the nuclear family: The increasing importance of multigenerational bonds, *Journal of Marriage and Family* 63, 1, 1–16

Bengston, V, Giarrusso, R, Mabry, JB, Silverstein, M, 2002, Solidarity, conflict and ambivalence: Complementary or competing perspectives on intergenerational relationships, *Journal of Marriage and Family* 64, 568–76

Benson, M, 2010, The context and trajectory of lifestyle migration, *European Societies* 12, 1, 45–64

Benson, M, 2011a, *The British in rural France: Lifestyle migration and the ongoing quest for a better way of life*, Manchester: Manchester University Press

Benson, M, 2011b, The movement beyond (lifestyle) migration: Mobile practices and the constitution of a better way of life, *Mobilities* 6, 2, 221–35

Benson, M, 2012, How culturally significant imaginings are translated into lifestyle migration, *Journal of Ethnic and Migration Studies* 38, 10, 1681–96

Benson, M, O'Reilly, K (eds), 2009, *Lifestyle migration: Expectations, aspirations and experiences*, Farnham: Ashgate

Benson, M, Osbaldiston, N (eds), 2014, *Understanding lifestyle migration: Theoretical approaches to migration and the quest for a better way of life*, Basingstoke: Palgrave Macmillan

Beshers, J, 1967, *Popluation processes in social systems*, New York: Free Press

Billig, M, 1995, *Banal nationalism*, London: Sage Publications

Blaakilde, AL, Nilsson, G (eds), 2013, *Nordic seniors on the move: Mobility and migration in later life*, Lund: Lund University

Blaikie, N, 1999, *Approaches to social enquiry*, Cambridge: Blackwell

Blokland, T, 2003, *Urban bonds: Social relationships in an inner city neighbourhood*, Cambridge: Polity Press

Borkert, M, Perez, AM, Scott, S, De Tona, C, 2006, Introduction: Understanding migration research (across national and academic boundaries) in Europe, *Forum: Qualitative Social Research* 7, 3, www.qualitative-research.net

Bonnett, A, 2000, *Anti-racism*, London: Routledge

Booker, C, 2004, *The seven basic plots: Why we tell stories*, New York: Continuum

Bourdieu, P, 1977, *Outline of a theory of practice*, Cambridge: Cambridge University Press

Bourdieu, P, 1984, *Distinction: A social critique of the judgment of taste*, Cambridge, MA: Harvard University Press

Bourdieu, P, 1986, The forms of capital, in JG Richardson (ed) *Handbook for theory and research for the sociology of education*, New York: Greenwood Press, 241–58

Boyd, M, Grieco, E, 2003, Women and migration: Incorporating gender into international migration theory, www.migrationinformation.org

Boym, S, 2001, *The future of nostalgia*, New York: Basic Books

Brah, A, 1996, *Cartographies of diaspora: Contesting identities*, London and New York: Routledge

Brannen, J, 2003, Towards a typology of intergenerational relations: Continuities and change in families, *Sociological Research Online* 8, 2, www.socresonline.org.uk

Brown, G, Yule, G, 1983, *Discourse analysis*, Cambridge: Cambridge University Press

Brown, M, 2012, Gender and sexuality: Intersectional anxieties, *Progress in Human Geography* 36, 4, 541–50

Bruner, JS, 1990, *Acts of meaning*, Cambridge, MA: Harvard University Press

Byrne, B, 2007, England – whose England? Narratives of nostalgia, emptiness and evasion in imaginations of national identity, *The Sociological Review*, 55, 3, 509–30

Calhoun, C, 1991, Indirect relationships and imagined communities, in P Bourdieu, JS Coleman (eds) *Social theory for a changing society*, Boulder, CO: Westview

Casado-Díaz, MA, 2006, Retiring to Spain: An analysis of differences among North European nationals, *Journal of Ethnic and Migration Studies* 32, 8, 1321–39

Casado-Díaz, MA, 2009, Social capital in the sun: Bonding and bridging social capital among British retirees, in M Benson, K O'Reilly (eds) *Lifestyle migration: Expectations, aspirations and experiences*, Farnham: Ashgate

Casado-Díaz, MA, Kaiser, C, Warnes, AM, 2004, Northern European retired residents in nine southern European areas: Characteristics, motivations and adjustment, *Ageing and Society* 24, 353–81

Castles, S, 2010, Understanding global migration: A social transformation perspective, *Journal of Ethnic and Migration Studies* 36, 10, 1565–86

Chaitin, J, Linstroth, JP, Hiller, PT, 2009, Ethnicity and belonging: An overview of a study of Cuban, Haitian and Guatemalan immigrants to Florida, *Forum: Qualitative Social Research Volume*, 10, 3

Chant, S, Radcliffe, S, 1992, Migration and development: The importance of gender, in S Chant (ed) *Gender and migration in developing countries*, 1–29, New York: Belhaven Press

Charmaz, K, 1993, The grounded theory method: An explication and interpretation, in RM Emerson (ed) *Contemporary field research: Perspectives and formulations*, Prospect Heights, IL: Waveland Press

Charmaz, K, 1995, Grounded theory, in J Smith, R Harre, L Langenhove (eds) *Rethinking methods in psychology*, London: Sage

Cherlin, A, Furstenberg, FF, 1985, Styles and strategies of grandparenting, in VL Bengston, JF Robertson (eds) Grandparenthood, Beverly Hills, CA: Sage

Cherlin, A, Furstenberg, FF, 1986, *The new American grandparent: A place in the family, a life apart*, Cambridge, MA: Harvard University Press, 1992

Cherlin, A, Furstenberg, F, 1992, *The new American grandparent: A place in the family, life apart*, New York, NY: Basic Books

Clark, A, 2007, Understanding community, *Real Life Methods Working Paper*, Leeds: Leeds University

Cohen, AP, 1982, *Belonging: Identity and social organisation in British rural cultures*, Manchester: Manchester University Press

Cohen, AP, 1985, *The symbolic construction of community*, London: Routledge

Coleman, D, 1990, *Foundations of social theory*, Cambridge, MA: Harvard University Press

Coleman, D, 1998, Social capital in the creation of human capital, *Journal of Sociology* 94, 95–120

Colombo, M, 2003, Reflexivity and narratives in action research: A discursive approach, *Forum: Qualitative Social Research* 4, 2, www.qualitative-research.net

Connidis, IA, McMullin, JA, 2002, Sociological ambivalence and family ties: A critical perspective, *Journal of Marriage and Family* 64, 3, 558–67

Conway, S, 2003, Ageing and imagined community: Some cultural constructions and reconstructions, *Sociological Research Online* 8, 2, www.socresonline.org.uk

Crenshaw, K, 1989, Demarginalizing the intersection of race and sex: A black feminist critique of antidiscrimination doctrine, feminist theory, and antiracist politics, *University of Chicago Legal Forum* 140, 139–67

Crenshaw, K, Gotanda, N, Peller, G, Kendall, T, 1995, *Critical race theory: the key writings that formed the movement*, New York, NY: The New Press

Cronin, N, 2006, *Translation and identity*, London: Routledge

Crow, G, 2002a, Community studies: Fifty years of theorization, *Sociological Research Online* 7, 3, www.socresonline.org.uk

Crow, G, 2002b, *Social solidarities: Theories and social change*, Buckingham, PA: Open University Press

Crow, G, Mah, A, 2012, *Research report: Conceptualisations and meanings of 'community': The theory and operationalisation of a contested concept*, www.community-methods.soton.ac.uk, Southampton: University of Southampton

Crow, G, Allan, G, Summers, M, 2001, Changing perspectives on the insider/outsider distinction in community sociology, *Community, Work and Family* 4, 1, 29–48

Crow, G, Allan, G, Summers, M, 2002, Neither busybodies nor nobodies: Managing proximity and distance in neighbourly relations, *Sociology* 36, 1, 127–45

Czarniawska, B, 2004, *Narratives in social science research*, London: Sage

Davidson, AP, Kuah-Pearce, KE, 2008, *At home in the Chinese diaspora: Memories, identities and belongings*, Basingstoke: Macmillan

Davies, B, Harre, R, 1990, Positioning: The social construction of selves, *Journal for the Theory of Social Behaviour* 20, 1, 43–63

Day, E, 2002, Me, my*self and I: Personal and professional re-constructions in ethnographic research, *Forum: Qualitative Social Research* 3, 3, www.qualitative-research.net

Day Sclater, S, 1998a, Nina's story: An exploration into the construction and transformation of subjectives in narrative accounting, *Auto/Biography* 6, 1 and 2, 67–77

Day Sclater, S, 1998b, Creating the self: Stories as transitional phenomena, *Auto/Biography* 6, 1 and 2, 85–92

De Haas, H, 2010, The internal dynamics of migration processes: A theoretical inquiry, *Journal of Ethnic and Migration Studies* 36, 10, 1587–617

De La Paz, PT, White, M, 2012, Fundamental drivers of house price change: The role of money, mortgages and migration in Spain and the United Kingdom, *Journal of Property Research* 29, 4, 341–67

Delanty, G, 1996, Beyond the nation-state: National identity and citizenship in a multicultural society – a response to rex, *Sociological Research Online* 1, 3, www.socresonline.org.uk

Delanty, G, 2003, *Community*, London: Routledge

Dench, G, Gavron, K, Young, M, 2006, *The new East End: Kinship, race and conflict*, Exmouth: Profile Books

Derrida, J, 1967, *Of grammatology*, translated by GC Spivak, Baltimore, MD: John Hopkins University Press

Dickinson, H, Erben, M, 2006, Nostalgia and autobiography: The past and the present, *Auto/Biography* 14, 3, 223–44

Didero, M, 2011, Media images and everyday realities: German-Moroccan perspectives on translocational positionalities, Paper presented at the International RC21 conference, Session 28, Living with Difference Round Table 2: Diversity and Social Cohesion, 7-9 July, Amsterdam

Doucet, A, Mauthner, NS, 2008, What can be known and how? Narrated subjects and the listening guide, *Forum: Qualitative social research* 8, 3, 399–409

Dudrah, R, 2004, Diasporicity in the city of Portsmouth (UK): Local and global connections of Black Britishness, *Sociological Research Online*, 9, 2, www.socresonline.org.uk/9/2/dudrah.html

Du Gay, P, Evans, J, Redman, P (eds), 2000, *Identity: A reader*, London: Sage

Duncan, T, Scott, A, Thulemark, M (eds), 2013, *Lifestyle mobilities: Intersections of travel, leisure and migration*, Farnham: Ashgate

Durkheim, E, [1877] 1989, *Suicide: A study in sociology* (translated by JA Spaulding, G Simpson) London, Routledge

Edwards, R, Franklin, J, Holland, J, 2003, *Families and Social Capital: Exploring the Issues*, London: South Bank University

Elias, N, 1974, Towards a theory of communities, in C Bell, H Newby (eds) *The sociology of community: A selection of readings*, pp ix–xli, London: Frank Cass

Elias, N. Scotson, JL, 1994, *The established and the outsiders* (2nd ed), London: Sage

Elliott, A, Urry, J, 2010, *Mobile lives*, Abingdon: Taylor and Francis

England, KVL, 1994, Getting personal: Reflexivity, positionality, and feminist research, *Professional Geographer* 46, 1, 80–9

Etzioni, A, 1995, *The spirit of community: Rights, responsibilities and the communitarian agenda*, London: Fontana Press

Finch, J, 1986, Age: An introduction, in RG Burgess (ed) *Key variables in social investigation*, London: Routledge

Finlay, L, 2002, 'Outing' the researcher: The provenance, process, and practice of reflexivity, *Qualitative Health Research* 12, 4, 531–45

Flint, J, Robinson, D (eds), 2008, *Community cohesion in crisis? New dimensions of diversity and difference*, Bristol: Policy Press

Frank, AW, 2000, The standpoint of the storyteller, *Qualitative Health Research* 10, 3, 354–65

Franklin, J, 2004, *Politics, trust and networks: Social capital in critical perspective*, London: London South Bank University

Fuss, D, 1989, *Essentially speaking: Feminism, nature and difference*, London, New York: Routledge

Ganga, D, Scott, S, 2006, Cultural 'insiders' and the issue of positionality in qualitative migration research: Moving 'across' and moving 'along' researcher–participant divides, *Forum: Qualitative Social Research* 7, 3, www.qualitative-research.net

Geoffrey, C, Sibley, R (eds), 2007, *Going abroad. Travel, tourism and migration: Cross cultural perspectives on mobility*, Cambridge: Scholars Publishing

Giddens, A, 1986, *The constitution of society: Outline of the theory of structuration*, Berkeley and Los Angeles, CA: University of California Press

Giddens, A, 1991, *Modernity and self-identity*, Palo Alto, CA: Stanford University Press

Giguere, N, 2013, 'Westerners' in Varanasi, India: A permanent yet temporary community, in M Korpela, F Dervin (eds) *Cocoon communities: Togetherness in the 21st century*, pp 15–36, Newcastle: Cambridge Scholars Publishing

Gillies, V, Edwards, R, 2006, A qualitative analysis of parenting and social capital: Comparing the work of Coleman and Bourdieu, *Qualitative Sociology Review* 2, 2, 42–60

Ginsburg, FD, 1989, Dissonance and harmony: The symbolic function of abortion in activists' life stories, in Personal Narratives Group (eds) *Interpreting women's lives: Feminist theory and personal narratives*, pp 59–84, Indianapolis, IN: Indiana University Press

Glaser, BG, Strauss, AL, 1967, *The discovery of grounded theory: Strategies for qualitative research*, New York: Aldine Publishing Company

Glick-Schiller, N, Basch, L, Szanton, B, 1995, *Immigrant to transmigrant: Theorizing transnational migration*, Institute for Ethnographic Research, Washington, DC, George Washington University

Goffman, E, 1959, *The presentation of self in everyday life*, Harmondsworth: Penguin

Goffman, E, 1975, *Frame analysis: An essay on the organisation of experience*, Harmondsworth: Penguin

Goffman, E, 1981, Footing, in E Goffman (ed) *Forms of talk*, pp 124–59, Philadelphia, PA: University of Pennsylvania Press

Grace, AP, Cavanagh, F, Ennis-Williams, C, Wells, C, 2006, Researchers' positionalities and experiences mediating lesbian, gay, bisexual, trans-identified and queer research as a personal and cultural practice, *Auto/Biography* 14, 4, 339–58

Gray, A, 2005, The changing availability of grandparents as carers and its implications for childcare policy in the UK, *Journal of Social Policy* 34, 4, 557–77

Greer, S, 1987, The community of limited liability, in P Worsley (ed) *The new modern sociology readings*, London: Penguin Books

Guberman, N, Lavoie, J-P, Blein, L, Olazabal, I, 2011, Baby-boomers and the 'denaturalisation' of care-giving in Quebec, *Ageing and Society* 31, 7, 1141–58

Gubrium, JF, Holstein, JA, 1998, Narrative practice and the coherence of personal stories, *The Sociological Quarterly* 39, 163–87

Gubrium, JF, Holstein, JA, 2009, *Analyzing narrative reality*, Thousand Oaks, CA: Sage

Gustafson, P, 2008, Transnationalism in retirement migration: The case of North European retirees in Spain, *Ethnic and Racial Studies* 31, 3, 451–75

Halfacree, K, 2012, Heterolocal identities? Counter-urbanisation, second homes, and rural consumption in the era of mobilities, *Population, Space and Place* 18, 209–24

Halfacree, K, 2014, Jumping up from the armchair: Beyond the idyll in counterurbanisation, in M Benson, N Osbaldiston (eds) *Understanding lifestyle migration: Theoretical approaches to migration and the quest for a better way of life*, Basingstoke: Palgrave Macmillan, 1–26,

Halfacree, K, Boyle, P, 1993, The challenge facing migration research: The case for a biographical approach, *Progress in Human Geography* 17, 3, 333–48

Hall, S, 2000, *Who needs identity?*, in P Du Gay, J Evans, P Redman (eds) *Identity: A reader*, London: Sage

Hardill, I, 2006, Presentation at CRESR, Sheffield Hallam University, April 2006

Harding, J, 2006, Questioning the subject in biographical interviewing, *Sociological Research Online*, 11, 3, www.socresonline.org.uk/11/3/harding.html

Harvey, D, 1989, *The condition of postmodernity*, Oxford: Blackwell

Hatch, JA, Wismiewski, R, 1995, *Life history and narrative: Questions, issues and exemplary works*, London: Talmer Press

Herlofson, K, Hagestad, GO, 2012, Transformations in the role of grandparents across welfare states, in S Arber, V Timonen (eds) *Contemporary grandparenting: Changing family relationships in global contexts*, Bristol: Policy Press

Hickman, MJ, Morgan, S, Walter, B, Bradley, J, 2005, The limitations of whiteness and the boundaries of Englishness: Second-generation Irish identifications and positionings in multiethnic Britain, *Ethnicities* 5, 2, 160–82

Hillery, G, 1955, Definitions of community: Areas of agreement, *Rural Sociology* 20, 111–23

Hoang, LA, 2011, Gender identity and agency in migration decision-making: Evidence from Vietnam, *Journal of Ethnic and Migration Studies* 37, 9, 1441–57

Hoggett, P, 1997, Contested communities, in P Hoggett (ed) *Contested communities: Experiences, struggles and policies*, Bristol: Policy Press

Holloway, SL, 2007, Burning issues: Whiteness, rurality and the politics of difference, *Geoforum* 38, 1, 7–20

Holstein, JA, Gubrium, JF, 2000, *The self we live by: Narrative identity in a postmodern world*, New York: Oxford University Press

Huber, A, O'Reilly, K, 2004, The construction of *Heimat* under conditions of individualised modernity: Swiss and British elderly migrants in Spain, *Ageing and Society* 24, 3, 327–52

Huete, R, 2009, *Turistas que llegan Para Quedarse: Una Explicación Sociológica Sobre la Movilidad Residencial*, Alicante: Publicaciones Universidad de Alicante

Huete, R, Mantecon, A, 2012, Residential tourism or lifestyle migration: Social Problems linked to the non-definition of the situation', in O Moufakkir, P Burns (eds) *Controversies in tourism*, Wallingford: CABI

Huete, R, Mantecon, A, Mazón, T, 2008, Analysing the social perception of residential tourism development, in C Costa, P Cravo (eds) *Advances in Tourism Research*, Aveiro: IASK

Huete, R, Mantecon, A, Estevez, J, 2013, Challenges in lifestyle migration research: Reflections and findings about the Spanish crisis, *Mobilities* 8, 3, 331–48

Janoschka, M, 2011, Between mobility and mobilization: Lifestyle migration and the practice of European identity in political struggles, *Sociological Review* 58, 270–90

Karn, VA, 1977, *Retiring to the seaside*, London and Boston: Routledge and Kegan Paul

King, R, 2002, Towards a new map of European migration, *International Journal of Population Geography* 8, 2, 89–106

King, R, 2012a, Geography and migration studies: Retrospect and prospect, *Population, Space and Place* 18, 2, 134–53

King, R, 2012b, Theories and typologies of migration: An overview and a primer, *Willy Brandt Series of Working Papers in International Migration and Ethnic Relations* 3, 12

King, R, Skeldon, R, 2010, 'Mind the gap!' Integrating approaches to internal and international migration, *Journal of Ethnic and Migration Studies* 36, 10, 1619–46

King, R, Smith, DP, 2012, Editorial introduction: Re-making migration theory, *Population, Space and Place*, 18, 2, 127–33

King, R, Warnes, AM, Williams AM, 1998, International retirement migration in Europe, *International Journal of Population Geography* 4, 2, 91–111

King, R, Warnes, T, Williams, A, 2000, *Sunset lives: British retirement migration to the Mediterranean*, Oxford: Berg

Knox, AB, 1977, *Adult development and learning*, San Francisco, CA: Jossey Bass

Ko, LSF, 2012, Solidarity, ambivalence and multi-generational co-residence in Hong Kong, in S Arber, V Timonen (eds) *Contemporary grandparenting: Changing family relationships in global contexts*, Bristol: Policy Press

Korpela, M, Dervin, F, 2013, *Cocoon communities: Togetherness in the 21st century*, Newcastle: Cambridge Scholars Publishing

Ladino, C, 2002, 'You make yourself sound so important': Fieldwork experiences, identity construction and non-Western researchers abroad, *Sociological Research Online* 7, 4, www.socresonline.org.uk

Lemos, G, Young, M, 1997, *The communities we have lost and can regain*, London: Lemos and Crane

Levitt, P, 2012, What's wrong with migration scholarship? A critique and a way forward, *Identities: Global studies in culture and power* 19, 4, 493–500

Levitt, P, Glick Schiller, N, 2004, Conceptualizing simultaneity: A transnational social field perspective on society, *International Migration Review* 38, 3, 1002–39

Lowenstein, A, Katz, R, Biggs, S, 2011, Rethinking theoretical and methodological issues in intergenerational family relations research, *Ageing and Society* 31, 7, 1077–83

Lundstrom, C, 2014, *White migrations: Gender, whiteness and privilege in transnational migration*, Basingstoke: Palgrave Macmillan

Lüscher, K. (2000) Ambivalence: A key concept for the study of intergenerational relations, in S Trnka (ed) *Family issues between gender and generations: Seminar report*, Vienna: European Observatory on Family Matters

Lüscher, K, Pillemer, K, 1998, Intergenerational ambivalence: A new approach to the study of parent–child relations in later life, *Journal of Marriage and Family* 60, 2, 413–45

Lutz, H, 2010, Gender in the migratory process, *Journal of Ethnic and Migration Studies* 36, 10, 1647–63

McAdams, DP, 1993, *The stories we live by: Personal myths and the making of the self*, New York: Guilford Press

McCall, L, 2005, The complexity of intersectionality, *Signs* 30, 3, 1771–800

MacCannell, D, 1973, Staged authenticity: Arrangements of social space in tourist settings, *American Journal of Sociology* 79, 3, 589–603

MacCannell, D, 1992, *Empty meeting grounds: The tourist papers*, London: Psychology Press

McDonald, L, 2011, Theorising about ageing, family and immigration, *Ageing and Society* 31, 7, 1180–201

McGhee, D, 2005, Patriots of the future? A critical examination of community cohesion strategies in contemporary Britain, *Sociological Research Online* 10, 3, www.socresonline.org.uk

MacIver, RM, Page, CH, 1961, *Society: An introductory analysis*, London: Macmillan

Maclennan, D, 2000, *Changing places, engaging people*, York, Joseph Rowntree Foundation

Mah, A, Crow, G, 2011, *Researching community in the 21st century: An annotated bibliography*, www.community-methods.soton.ac.uk, Southampton: University of Southampton

Manalansan IV, MF, 2006, Queer intersections: Sexuality and gender in migration studies, *International Migration Qualitative Health Research* 16, 10, 1317–34

Mann, R, 2006, Reflexivity and researching national identity, *Sociological Research Online* 11, 4, www.socresonline.org.uk

Mantecon, A, Huete, R, 2007, The role of authenticity in tourism planning: Empirical findings from southeast Spain, *Tourism Review* 55, 3, 323–33

Marsh, P, Bradley, S, Love, C, Alexander, P, Norham, R, 2007, *Belonging*, Research commissioned by The Automobile Association, Oxford: The Social Issues Research Centre

Maslow, AH, 1943, A theory of human motivation, *Psychological Review*, 50, 370–96

Mason, J, 2002, *Qualitative researching*, London: Sage

Massey, DS, Arango, J, Hugo, G, Kouaouci, A, Pellegrino, A, Taylor, JE, 1998, *Worlds in motion*, Oxford: Clarendon Press

May, V, 2004, *Lone motherhood in historical context: Changing elements in narrative identity*, Huddersfield: University of Huddersfield Press

May, V, 2008, On being a 'good' mother: The moral presentation of self in written life stories, *Sociology* 42, 3, 470–85

May, V, 2013, *Connecting self to society: Belonging in a changing world*, Basingstoke: Palgrave Macmillan

May, V, Mason, J, Clarke, L, 2012, Being there yet not interfering: The paradoxes of grandparenting, in S Arber, V Timonen (eds) *Contemporary grandparenting: Changing family relationships in global contexts,* Bristol: Policy Press

Merton, RK, 1972, Insiders and outsiders: A chapter in the sociology of knowledge, *American Journal of Sociology, Varieties of Political Expression in Sociology* 78, 1, 9–47

Mills, CW, 1940, Situated actions and vocabularies of motive, *American Sociological Review* 5, 6, 439–52

Mills, CW, 1959, *The sociological imagination*, New York, NY: Oxford University Press

Milner, LM, 1968, Factors influencing admission to a community mental health center, *Community Mental Health* 4, 1, 27–35

Mooney, G, Neal, S (eds), 2008, *Community: Welfare, crime and society*, Maidenhead: Open University Press

Morse, JM, 1994, Designing funded qualitative research, in NK Denzin, YS Lincoln (eds) *Handbook of qualitative research*, Thousand Oaks, CA: Sage

Morse, JM, 1999, Qualitative generalizability, *Qualitative Health Research* 9, 1, 5–6

Morse, JM, 2004, Constructing qualitatively-derived theory: Concept construction and concept typologies, *Qualitative Health Research* 14, 10, 1387–95

Murray, M, 2000, Social capital formation and health communities: Insights from the Colorado Healthy Eating Communities Initiative, *Community Development Journal* 35, 2, 99–108

Nagy, R, Korpela, M, 2013, Introduction: Limitations to temporary mobility, *International Review of Social Research* 3, 1, 1–6

Neugarten, BL, Weinstein, KK, 1964, The changing American grandparent, *Journal of Marriage and the Family* 45, 267–76

Newby, H, 1980, *Green and pleasant land?*, Harmondsworth: Penguin

Nilsson, G, 2013, Breaking free and settling down: Contradictory cultural meanings of rural retirement migration among Swedish seniors, in AL Blaakilde, G Nilsson (eds) *Nordic seniors on the move: Mobility and migration in later life*, pp 27–50, Lund: Lund University

O'Reilly, K, 2000a, *The British on the Costa del Sol: Transnational identities and local communities*, London and New York: Routledge

O'Reilly, K, 2000b, Trading intimacy for liberty: British women on the Costa del Sol, in F Anthias, G Lazaridis, *Gender and migration in Southern Europe*, Oxford: Berg, 227–48

O'Reilly, K, 2002, Britain in Europe/the British in Spain: exploring Britain's changing relationship to the other through the attitudes of its emigrants, *Nations and Nationalism*, 8, 2, 179–93

O'Reilly, K, 2003, When is a tourist?: The articulation of tourism and migration in Spain's Costa del Sol, *Tourist Studies* 3, 3, 301–17

O'Reilly, K, 2007a, Emerging tourism futures: Residential tourism and its implications, in C Geoffroy, R Sibley (eds) *Going abroad: Travel, tourism and migration. Cross-cultural perspectives on mobility*, Newcastle: Cambridge Scholars Publishing

O'Reilly, K, 2007b, Intra-European migration and the mobility-enclosure dialectic, *Sociology* 41, 2, 277–93

O'Reilly, K, 2012, *International migration and social theory*, Houndmills: Palgrave

O'Reilly, K, 2014, The role of the social imaginary in lifestyle migration: Employing the ontology of practice theory, in M Benson, N Osbaldiston (eds) *Understanding lifestyle migration: Theoretical approaches to migration and the quest for a better way of life*, pp 211–34, Basingstoke: Palgrave Macmillan

O'Reilly, K, Benson, M, 2009, Lifestyle migration: Escaping to the good life?, in M Benson, K O'Reilly (eds) *Lifestyle migration: Expectations, aspirations and experiences*, Farnham: Ashgate

Oliver, C, 2008, *Retirement migration: Paradoxes of ageing*, New York: Routledge

Oliver, C, O'Reilly, K, 2010, A Bourdieusian analysis of class and migration: Habitus and the individualising process, *Sociology* 44, 1, 49–66

Osbaldiston, N, 2014, Beyond ahistoricity and mobilities in lifestyle migration research, in M Benson, N Osbaldiston (eds) *Understanding lifestyle migration: Theoretical approaches to migration and the quest for a better way of life*, pp 163–87, Basingstoke: Palgrave Macmillan

Pahl, RE, 1966, The rural–urban continuum, *Sociologia Ruralis* 6, 3, 299–327

Papastergiadis, N, 2000, *The turbulence of migration: Globalization, deterritorialization and hybridity*, Cambridge: Polity Press

Perez, AM, 2006, Doing qualitative research with migrants as a native citizen: Reflections from Spain, *Forum: Qualitative Social Research* 7, 3, www.qualitative-research.net

Phillips, T, 2002, Imagined communities and self-identity: An exploratory quantitative analysis, *Sociology* 36, 3, 597–617

Phillipson, C, 2007, The 'elected' and the 'excluded': Sociological perspectives on the experience of place and community in old age, *Ageing and Society* 27, 3, 321–42

Phillipson, C, Leach, R, Money, A, Biggs, S, 2008, Social and cultural constructions of ageing: The case of the baby boomers, *Sociological Research Online* 13, 3, www.socresonline.org.uk

Plummer, K, 2001, *Documents of life 2: An invitation to critical humanism*, London: Sage

Polanyi, L, 1985, *Telling the American story: A structural and cultural analysis of conversational storytelling*, Norwood: Ablex

Polkinghorne, DE, 1988, *Narrative knowing and the Human Sciences*, Albany: State University of New York Press

Putnam, RD, 1993, *Making democracy work: Civil traditions in modern Italy*, Princeton, NJ: Princeton University Press

Putnam, RD, 2000, *Bowling alone: The collapse and revival of American community*, New York: Simon and Schuster

Ravenstein, EG, 1885, The laws of migration, *Journal of the Statistical Society of London*, 48, 2

Rex, J, 1996, Contemporary nationalism, its causes and consequences for Europe: A reply to Delanty, *Sociological Research Online* 1, 4, www.socresonline.org.uk

Rhodes, C, 1996, Researching organisational change and learning: A narrative approach, *The Qualitative Report* 2, 4, www.nova.edu/ssss/QR/QR2-4/rhodes.html

Ricoeur, P, 1984, *Time and narrative Vol 1*, Chicago, IL: Chicago University Press

Ricoeur, P, 1985, *Time and narrative Vol 2*, Chicago, IL: Chicago University Press

Ricoeur, P, 1988, *Time and narrative Vol 3*, Chicago, IL: Chicago University Press

Riessman, CK, 1990a, *Divorce talk: Women and men make sense of personal relationships*, New Brunswick, NJ: Rutgers University Press

Riessman, CK, 1990b, Strategic uses of narrative in the presentation of self and illness, *Social Science and Medicine* 30, 11, 1195–200

Riessman, CK, 1990c, *Strategic uses of narrative in the presentation of self and illness: A research note*, Oxford: Pergamon Press

Riessman, CK, 1993, *Narrative analysis (qualitative research methods)*, Thousand Oaks, CA: Sage

Riessman, CK, 2000a, Analysis of personal narratives, in N Denzin, Y Lincoln (eds) *Handbook of qualitative research*, Thousand Oaks, CA: Sage

Riessman, CK, 2000b, Even if we don't have children [we] can live: Stigma and infertility in South India, in C Mattingly, L Garro (eds) *Narratives and the cultural construction of illness and healing*, Berkeley, CA: University of California Press

Riessman, CK, 2003, Performing identities in illness narrative: Masculinity and multiple sclerosis, *Qualitative Research*, 3, 1

Riessman, CK, 2005, Narrative analysis, in *Narrative, memory and everyday life*, Huddersfield: University of Huddersfield, 1–7

Riessman, CK, 2008, *Narrative methods for the human sciences*, London: Sage

Roberts, B, 2002, *Biological research*, Buckingham: Open University Press

Roberts, B, 2004, Political activism and narrative analysis: The biographical template and the meat pot, *Forum: Qualitative Social Research* 5, 3, www.qualitative-research.net

Roberts, B, 2008, Performative social science: A consideration of skills, purpose and context, *Forum: Qualitative Social Research* 9, 2, www.qualitative-research.net

Rodriguez, V, Fernández-Mayoralas, G, Rojo, F, 1998, European retirees on the Costa del Sol: A cross-national comparison, *International Journal of Population Geography* 4, 183–200

Rowe, JW, Kahn, RL, 1997, Successful aging, *The Gerontologist* 37, 4, 433–40, doi:10.1093/geront/37.4.433

Ryan, L, 2004, *Family matters: (E)migration, familial networks and Irish women in Britain*, Oxford: Blackwell

Ryan, L, Webster, W (eds), 2008, *Gendering migration: Masculinity, femininity and ethnicity in post-war migration to Britain*, Farnham: Ashgate

Rye, JF, 2006, Rural youths' images of the rural, *Journal of Rural Studies* 22, 4, 409–21

Salazar, NB, 2014, Migrating imaginaries of a better life…until paradise finds you, in M Benson, N Osbaldiston (eds) *Understanding lifestyle migration: Theoretical approaches to migration and the quest for a better way of life*, pp 119–38, Basingstoke: Palgrave Macmillan

Sandel, TL, Cho, GE, Miller, PJ, Wang, S-H, 2006, What it means to be a grandmother: A cross-cultural study of Taiwanese and Euro-American grandmothers' beliefs, *Journal of Family Communication* 6, 4, 255–78

Savage, M, Bennett, T, 2005, Editors' introduction: Cultural capital and social inequality, *British Journal of Sociology* 56, 1, 1–12

Savage, M, Bagnall, G, Longhurst, B, 2001, Ordinary, ambivalent and defensive: Class identities in the northwest of England, *Sociology* 35, 4, 875–92

Schick, R, 2002, When the subject is difference: Conditions of voice in policy- orientated qualitative research, *Qualitative Inquiry* 8, 5, 632–51

Seeley, JR, Sim, RA, Loosley, EW, 1956, *Crestwood Heights*, New York: Basic Books

Seymour-Davies, H, 1996, *Bottle-brush tree: Village in Andalusia*, London: Black Swan

Sherlock, K, 2002, Community matters: Reflections from the field, *Sociological Research Online* 7, 2, www.socresonline.org.uk.uk

Shotter, J, 1984, *Social accountability and selfhood*, Oxford: Blackwell

Skeggs, B, 1997, *Formations of class and gender: Becoming respectable*, London: Sage

Skeggs, B, 2004, *Class, self, culture*, London: Routledge

Skey, M, 2011, *National belonging and everyday life: The significance of nationhood in an uncertain world*, Basingstoke: Palgrave Macmillan

Skrbiš, Z, 2008, Transnational families: Theorising migration, emotion and belonging, *Journal of Intercultural Studies* 29, 3, 231–46

Skultans, V, 1998, *The testimony of lives: Narratives and memory in post-Soviet Latvia*, London: Routledge

Smallwood, D, 2007, The integration of British migrants in Aquitaine, in C Geoffroy, R Sibley (eds) *Going abroad. Travel, tourism and migration: Cross cultural perspectives on mobility*, Cambridge: Scholars Publishing

Somers, MR, 1994, The narrative constitution of identity: A relational and network approach, *Theory and Society* 23, 5, 605–49

Song, M, Parker, D, 1995, Commonality, difference and the dynamics of disclosure in in-depth interviewing, *Sociology* 29, 2, 241–56

Spradley, JP, 1979, *The ethnographic interview*, New York: Holt, Rinehart and Winston

Stanley, L, Wise, S, 1990, Method, methodology and epistemology in feminist research processes, in L Stanley (ed) *Feminist praxis: Research, theory and epistemology in feminist sociology*, London: Routledge

Staunæs, D, 2010, Where have all the subjects gone? Bringing together the concepts of intersectionality and subjectification, *NORA (Nordic Journal of Feminist and Gender Research)* 11, 2, 101–10

Stones, R, 2005, *Structuration theory*, Basingstoke: Palgrave Macmillan

Suttles, G, 1972, *The social construction of community*, Chicago, IL: University of Chicago Press

Sweetman, P, 2003, Twenty-first century dis-ease? Habitual reflexivity or the reflexive habitus, *Sociological Review* 51, 4, 528–49

Tamboukou, M, 2008a, Re-imagining the narratable subject, *Qualitative Research* 8, 3, 283–92

Taylor, RC, 1969, Migration and motivation: a study of determinants and types, in JA Jackson, (ed) *Migration*, Cambridge: Cambridge University Press, 99–130

Temple, B, 1998, A fair trial? Judging quality in qualitative research, *International Journal of Social Research Methodology* 1, 3, 205–15

Temple, B, 1999, Diaspora space and polish women, *Women's Studies International Forum* 22, 1, 17–24

Temple, B, 2001, Polish families: A narrative approach, *Journal of Family Issues* 22, 3, 386–99

Temple, B, 2002, Crossed wires: Interpreters, translators and bilingual workers in cross language research, *Qualitative Health Research* 2, 6, 844–54

Temple, B, 2008a, Investigating language and Identity in cross-language narratives, *Migrations and Identities* 1, 1, 1–18

Temple, B, 2008b, Narrative analysis of written texts: Reflexivity in cross language research, *Qualitative Research* 8, 3, 355–65

Temple, B, Moran, R, Fayas, N, Haboninana, S, Mccabe, F, Mohamed, Z, Noori, A, Rahman, N, 2005, *Learning to live together: Developing communities with dispersed refugee people seeking asylum*, York: Joseph Rowntree Foundation

Thang, LL, Meheta, K, Usui, T, Tsuruwaka, M, 2011, Being a good grandparent: Roles and expectations in intergenerational relationships in Japan and Singapore, *Marriage and Family Review* 47, 8, 548–70

Timonen, V, Arber, S, 2012, A new look at grandparenting, in S Arber, V Timonen (eds) *Contemporary grandparenting: Changing family relationships in global contexts*, Bristol: Policy Press

Torkington, K, 2012, Place and lifestyle migration: The discursive construction of 'glocal' place-identity, *Mobilities* 7, 1, 71–92

Torres, S, 2004, Making sense of the construct of successful aging: The migrant experience, in SO Daatland, S Biggs (eds) *Aging and diversity: Multiple pathways and cultural migrations*, Bristol: Policy Press

Urry, J, 1990, *The tourist gaze: leisure and travel in contemporary societies*, London: Sage

Urry, J, 2000, Beyond the Science of 'Society', *Sociology* 36, 2, 255–74

Valentine, G, 2007, Theorizing and researching intersectionality: A challenge for feminist geography, *The Professional Geographer* 59, 1, 10–21

Van Hear, N, 2010, Theories of migration and social change, *Journal of Ethnic and Migration Studies* 36, 10, 1531–36

van Noorloos, FV, 2013, Residential tourism and multiple mobilities: Local citizenship and community fragmentation in Costa Rica, *Sustainability* 5, 570–89

Vertovec, S, 2010, Transnationalism and identity, *Journal of Ethnic and Migration Studies* 27, 4, 573–82

Wahl, H-W, Lang, FR, 2004, Aging in context across the adult lifecourse: Integrating physical and social environmental research perspectives, in HW Wahl, R Scheidt, P Windley (eds) *Focus on aging in context: Socio-physical environments*, Annual Review of Gerontology and Geriatrics 23, pp 1–33, New York: Springer Publishing Company

Waldren, J, 1996, *Insiders and outsiders: Paradise and reality in Mallorca*, New York: Berghahn

Warnes, AM, Patterson, G, 1998, British retirees in Malta: Components of the cross-national relationship, *International Journal of Population Geography* 4, 2, 113–33

Warnes, AM, Friedrich, K, Kellaher, L, Torres, S, 2004, The diversity and welfare of older migrants in Europe, *Ageing and Society* 24, 3, 307–26

Wetherell, M, Laflech, M, Berkeley, R, (eds), 2007, *Identity, ethnic diversity and community cohesion*, London: Sage

Wheelock, J, Jones, K, 2002, 'Grandparents are the next best thing': Informal childcare for working parents in urban Britain, *Journal of Social Policy* 31, 3, 441–63

Williams, AM, 2005, *International migration and knowledge*, Oxford: COMPAS (Centre on Migration, Policy and Society)

Williams, AM, Hall, CM, 2002, Tourism and migration: New relationships between production and consumption, *Tourism Geographies*, 2, 1, 5–27

Williams, AM, Patterson, G, 1998, 'An empire lost but a province gained': A cohort analysis of British international retirement in the Algarve, *International Journal of Population Geography* 4, 2, 135–55

Windance Twine, FW, Warren, J (eds), 2000, *Racing research researching race: Methodological dilemmas in critical race studies*, New York: New York University Press

Winter, I, 2000, Social capital and public policy in context, in I Winter (ed) *Social capital and public policy in Australia*, Melbourne: Australian Institute of Family Studies

Wood, D (ed), 1981, *On Paul Ricouer: Narrative and interpretation*, New York: Routledge

Woodward, K, ed, 2002, *Identity and difference*, London: Sage

Woolcock, M, 2001, The place of social capital in understanding social and economic outcomes, *Canadian Journal of Policy Research* 2, 1, 11–17

Woolcock, M, Narayan, D, 2000, Social capital: Implications for development theory, research and policy, *World Bank Research Observer* 15, 2, 225–49

Wright Mills, CW, 1940, Situated actions and vocabularies of motive, *American Sociological Review* 5, 6 (December), 904–9

Wright Mills, CW,1959, *The sociological imagination*, Oxford: Oxford University Press

Wright, P, 1985, *On living in an old country: The national past in contemporary Britain*, London: Verso

Yuval-Davis, N, Kannabiran, L, Vieten, V, 2006, *The situated politics of belonging*, London: Sage

Zlotnik, H, 2003, The global dimensions of female migration, *Migration information source*, www.migrationpolicy.org

Zontini, E, 2004, *Italian families and social capital: Rituals and the provision of care in British–Italian transnational families*, London: South Bank University

Index

A

adventure 46, 92–3
adventure time 27–8
  biographical disruption 71–3
  'random temporal contingencies' 27,
    65–6
affluence, *see* wealth
age
  gerontology theories
    agency and choice 40
    continuity theories 40
    disengagement theories 40
    women's positionality 39–40
agency, *see* human agency
alienation 84–5
  reasons for leaving the UK 80–4
ambivalence 9, 108–9, 129, 152–4
  belonging and 147
  family relations 141
  role as a grandmother 132–3, 138, 145
authenticity
  lack of 100–1

B

belonging
  alienation in the UK 80–5
  community and 54–5, 161, 163–4
    community of place 58–9
    constructing communities 57–8
    identity 60
    imagined communities 56
    networks 59–60
    positionality 60
  identificational belonging 60, 157–8
  locating 'home; 157–9
  regaining community in Spain 93–5
  see also dislocation; marginalisation
better way of life 51, 78–80
  obstacles
    hedonism 96
    living on *urbanizaciones* 97–103
    sharing space with holiday-makers 101
    temptations 95–6
  time spent with partners 109–11
boundaries 99
  belonging and boundaries 40, 51–2 108,
    111, 117
  identificational belonging 60

boundary spanning 51–2, 65, 105, 158
  community 51–2
  geographical 51
  language and 114–17
  tourism v migration 18
  'us' and 'them' 120–1, 126
  see also belonging; community

C

camaraderie 94–5, 106
cheap air travel 2, 37
  see also mass tourism
class 3, 22, 113–14
  networks and 105–6, 108, 126, 158
  ordinariness 42
  privilege 44, 45
  women's positionality 31, 33, 38, 41–7,
    50, 77, 85
climate 2, 68, 74–5, 90, 148–9
community 1, 13
  belonging and 54–5, 58, 161, 163–4
    community of place 58–9
    constructing communities 57–8
    identity 60
    imagined communities 56
    networks 59–60
    positionality 60
  boundaries and communities 51–2
  concept, community as a 52
    subjectivity 53
  loss of 94
    nostalgia 55–8
  nostalgia and 164
    restorative nostalgia 164–5
    reflective nostalgia 164–5
  physical context, community as a 53–4
  regaining 93–5
  search for
    motivation to migrate 53
  social change 53–4
  theoretical locus 54
  utopian idea, as a 161
cost of living 2, 35–6, 65, 67–8, 70, 74
contexts of decision-making 35
  mobility 37
structural contexts 35
  cultural context 35–6
  demographic context 35–6

opportunities 35
temporal context 35
counter-urbanisation 88

D

decision-making 70
agency 65, 70
family considerations 67, 77
types of decision-making 77–8
conflicted 74, 77
consensual 74–5
negotiated 74
uncontested 74, 75–6
disillusion 92, 123, 129, 154, 155–6, 157, 158
dislocation 1, 18, 54, 65–9, 78, 84–5, 152, 158, 165
translocation and 162–3
see also alienation; marginalisation

E

economic resources 36–7, 144–5, 150
Englishness 117–21
bridging and bonding social capital 118
Britishness distinguished from Englishness 117, 120–1
exclusion from 123–4
identification as the 'other' 120
lack of assimilation 121–3
obstacle to life in Spain, as an 121–3
'othering' the Spanish 124–6
positionality, as 121
escapism 1, 67–70, 88, 92, 103, 150–1, 153
ethnicity
as a positionality 40–1
European Union
enlargement 1–2, 37–8
freedom of movement 144

F

family 67, 70–1
missing the family 129, 144, 149–50
grand-parenting at distance 130–3
grandparents as distant figures 130
grandparents as formal 130
grandparents as fun-seekers 130
grandmother narratives 133–42
renegotiating family relationships 37, 39, 60, 73, 78, 129–30, 142–6
grand-parenting 130–3
fourth age 8, 152, 153
freedom 37, 39–40, 87, 91–2, 100, 103, 137–41, 143, 152
restrictions on
living on urbanizaciones 155–6
uncertainty and 163–4

freedom of movement 66, 144
Maastricht Treaty 36

G

gender
household gender dynamics
decision-making 73, 74–8, 150
increasing interest in migration experience 4
networks 70, 106, 111–14, 126
women's invisibility on map of migration 3–4
women's positionality 22, 31, 32–4, 39, 43–4, 49–50, 66, 85, 105–6, 158
globalisation
impact on migration 1–2, 37–8, 61
grand-parenting 130–3
constructing identities 144–5
distant figures 130
formal 130
fun-seekers 130
narratives 133–42
negotiating relationships 142–6
technological advances 131
solidarity 131–2
conflict and 132–3, 145–6
see also family

H

habitus 22, 41–2
health benefits 7
of migration, 68, 70, 74–6, 79, 96, 115, 151, 153–5
home
belonging 148, 151–2, 159–60
choosing to remain in Spain 147
agency 149–51
ambivalence 152–54
locating 'home' 147–60
Spain as 148–52
belonging 148, 151–2
quality of life 148
transmigrants 159
transnationalism 159
UK as 154–5, 156–7
disillusionment with Spain 155–6, 157
human agency 3, 10
decision-making 73
couples 74–5
single women 73–4
structure and 21–2, 38
see also decision-making

I

idealism 88–9, 103
identificational belonging 60, 157–8
identity
construction of Englishness

Britishness, distinguished from
117–18, 120
not-belonging 118
'otherness' 119
narrative and 29–31
see also positionality
idyllism 89–91
adventure, idyll as 92–3
freedom, idyll as 91–2
imagination 52, 55
alternative lifestyles 56
belonging and 56
constructing the idyll 158–9, 160
imagined communities 56
networks 60
nostalgia 158–60, 164
see also idyllism
imagined communities
belonging 56
individualisation 65, 74–8, 87, 126,
132–3, 138–39
family and 141, 144–5
integration 132, 157–8
cultural integration 158
identificational integration 157–8
interactive integration 158
networks 59
post-migration realities 125–6
structural integration 158
sustained family integration 134, 145
see also belonging; networks
international retirement migration 18, 20
conceptualisation 17–20
mobility 17–18
factors influencing 2
narration of 22–31
positionalities in 38–9
age 39–40
class 41–7
ethnicity 40–1
gender 39
structural contexts 35–8
see also individual headings

L

landscape 89–91, 103
language 118, 126
inability to speak Spanish 114–17
intention to learn Spanish 115
'otherness', contribution to 115
structure and agency, as 114
lifestyle migration 2
categories
bourgeois bohemians 19
residential tourists 19
rural idyll seekers 19
criticisms 19–20
definition 19

time/space dimension 19
linguistic ability 114–17

M

marginalisation, feelings of
age prejudice 80
government policy 80–1
immigration 81, 82–4
mass tourism 2–3, 37–8
Mediterranean idyll 2, 28, 87–8, 91–2,
103
migrants
categories 18
migration
categories 18
migration studies
biographical approach 9
context 10, 11–12
difficulties 21–2
experiences 11, 12–13
life-history approach 9
theories 20–2
cultural turn 20–1
difference over time 20
historical structural models 20
neo-classicism approaches 20
new economic theory 20
mobility 2, 17–18
modernisation 88, 98
modernity 119, 165
'loss' of community 1, 54–5, 88–9, 161
motivation
to migrate 65–6
better way of life 78–80
'the call' 67–8
cost of living 70
escape 67–9, 78–9
health benefits 70
quality of life 70, 78–9
weather 69, 79
choosing Spain 66
freedom of movement within the EU
66
joining family 67
previous tourist experience 66, 72
proximity to the UK 66–7
leaving the UK
age prejudice 80
government policy 80–1
immigration 81, 82–4
multiple motivations
'the call' 67–78
see also decision-making

N

narratives
analysis
content 32

change and movement over time and
place 22–3
construction of narratives 32–3
deconstruction of narratives 33
exercising of agency 22
exploring positionalities 22–3, 33
reflexivity of women 22, 47–8
approach to migration studies 9
capturing 31–2
counter-narratives, as 3, 33, 52, 118–19,
164
definition 10
identity construction and 29–31
interpretative nature 10, 163
plot and
narrative linkage 23–4
practices and outcomes in migration
23
social and cultural context 23
typologies 23
positionality and 29–31
time and 25–6
nostalgia 26–9
natural environment 89–91, 103
networks 105–6, 126–7
community bonding 59–60
depth of friendships 108–9
integration 157–8
'othering' the Spanish 124–6
importing cultural practices 125
partners 109–11
sense of belonging and 107
Silver Ladies Club 111–14
superficiality of relationships 108–9, 158
types of networks 106–7
UK and Spain compared
meaningful nature of relationships
108–9
see also social capital
non-belonging, see dislocation
nostalgia 1, 13
chronotopes 26–9, 57–8
adventure chronotopes 27–8
idyll chronotopes 28–9
community and 55, 164
constructing communities 57–8
imagined communities 56
reflective nostalgia 164–5
restorative nostalgia 164–5
constructing communities 57–8
homesickness 57, 148, 165
linking time and place 10, 26

O

otherness 41, 82–3
construction of Englishness 119
language and 115
'othering' the Spanish 124–6

importing cultural practices 125
time and place, of 89
see also self

P

place 162
community of place 58–9
narratives and 22–3
plot 10
narrative linkage 23–4
practices and outcomes in migration 23
social and cultural context 23
typologies 23
see also narratives
positionality 10, 38–9, 162
age 39–40, 80–1
alienation in the UK 80–5
class 41–7
Englishness/Britishness 117–21
ethnicity 40–1
cosmopolitanism 121
diaspora 121
hybridity 121
transnational belonging 121
gender 39
identity and 29–31
insider/outsider 48
intersectionality 29–30
performance and 30
subjectivity 30
translocational positionality 31
post-migration 3
disillusion 92, 123, 129, 154, 155–6,
157, 158
networks 59, 111–14

Q

quality of life 19, 37, 47, 65, 70, 96, 103,
148, 151 – 2, 160, 161

R

relationships, see families; networks; social
capital
residential categories
ambivalent about staying 9
living in Spain part of the year 9
wishing to remain 9
wishing to return 9
residential tourism 18–19, 20
retirement migration, see international
retirement migration
return migration 1, 153

S

sedimentation 81–2
self
other and 30, 40–1
see also identity

social capital
  networks and 111–14
    bridging and bonding 118
social change
  belonging and 52–5
  community and 52–5
  cultural 3
  demographic 3
  nostalgia 57, 164
  retirement migration as a consequence
    of, 53–4, 57
  structural 3
  uncertainty and 163–4
social field 41–2
structuration theory 21–2
structure
  agency and 21–2, 38
  contexts of decision-making 35
    cultural context 35–6
    demographic context 35–6
    mobility 37
    opportunities 35
    rejection of traditional values 37
    temporal context 35

T

tourists 101
  residential tourists 18–19, 98
  tourist space 105, 107
transmigrants 159
transnationalism 20, 121, 159

U

urbanizaciones 2
  committees 101–3
    corruption 102
    illusion of community 102–3
    marginalisation of women 102
  lack of authenticity 100–1
  networking 99
  reality of living on 97–8, 155–6
  remoteness 99
utopias 51, 88

W

wealth 36–7, 144–5
weather 2, 70, 90–1, 150